The Mini Book of Mini Darts

How to Play 43 Games, Plus Trivia, Lore, and More

By Randall Lotowycz and John Passineau

WORKMAN PUBLISHING, NEW YORK

To Tom, Anne, Laura, Chris, James,
Julia, Angela, Joe, Doug, Kara, Robbie, and Nate
—R. L.

For Virginia
—J. P.

We'd like to thank Margot Herrera and Heather Schwedel for their editorial insights, along with Beth Levy, Orlando Adiao, Melissa Lucier, Barbara Peragine, Doug Wolff, Phil Conigliaro, Kevin Williams, and John Duggan for their efforts and contributions. A special thanks to Suzie Bolotin and Peter Workman for their support over the years.

Text copyright © 2013 by Randall Lotowycz
Illustrations copyright © Workman Publishing Co., Inc.
Dartboard illustration on page 8 by Philip Hoffhines.
Dartboard illustration on page 10 by James Williamson.
All other dartboard illustrations by John Passineau.
Photo credits appear on p. 72.

Library of Congress Cataloging-in-Publication Data is available.

ISBN 978-0-7611-7743-2

Design by Orlando Adiao

Photo research by Melissa Lucier

Workman books are available at special discounts when purchased in bulk for premiums and sales promotions as well as for fund-raising or educational use. Special editions or book excerpts can also be created to specification. For details, contact the Special Sales Director at the address below, or send an email to specialmarkets@workman.com.

Workman Publishing Company, Inc.
225 Varick Street
New York, NY 10014-4381
workman.com

WORKMAN is a registered trademark of Workman Publishing Co., Inc.

Printed in China
First printing September 2013

10 9 8 7 6 5 4 3 2 1

Contents

Introduction: Darts 101 iv

The Dartboard Explained v

The Anatomy of a Dart v

The Perfect Throw vi

Darts Vocabulary vii

The Games 1

1. 501 2

2. Finnish Darts 4

3. Cricket 6

    BONUS GAME: Tactics 6

4. Shanghai 8

5. Fox Hunt 10

6. American Darts 12

    BONUS GAME: Strikeout 12

7. Mulligan 14

8. Over/Under 15

9. Shooting Hoops 16

10. Pyramid Power 18

11. Stonehenge Calling 20

12. Cupid's Arrow 22

13. Pinball 24

14. Pool 26

15. Bingo 27

16. The End of the World 28

17. Trip to the Stars 30

18. Office Wars 32

19. Passing Time 34

20. Battle at Sea 36

21. Record Player Revolution 38

22. Nine-Hole Golf 40

23. Battle of the Drums 42

24. The Beehive 44

25. Super Arcade Challenge 46

26. Bowling 48

27. Hockey Face-off 50

28. Football 52

29. Skee-Ball 54

30. Global Conqueror 55

31. Roulette 56

32. Raceway Melee 58

33. Knockdown 59

34. Please Stand By 60

35. Coney Island Hustle 62

36. Haunted House 63

37. Blackjack 64

    BONUS GAME: Poker 64

38. Picky Pizza 66

39. Boardwalk Juggling 68

40. Word on the Street 70

Additional Reading and Resources 72

◎ *Introduction: Darts 101*

Welcome to the weird and wild world of darts. It's a sport (and, yes, it really is a sport) that anyone can play, and it's popular all across the globe for that very reason. But don't expect to turn pro after a few simple throws. Patience and skill are necessary, and both come only with plenty of practice.

It used to be that practicing darts required a heavy board affixed to a wall that you wouldn't mind poking some holes into. But those days are gone: With this kit, you can take your boards with you and play anytime, anywhere. What follows are instructions for 43 darts games, some of which have been played for decades and others that were created specifically for this book. There are regulation games played in official competitions, variations on classic sports like baseball and basketball, games to play with office buddies, even games to play while you're waiting for your pizza to be delivered. Most include modifications to either increase or decrease the difficulty level.

In these pages, you'll also receive a crash course in the history of this relatively young sport. It rose to popularity primarily in the past 100 years. Its story is littered with common myths and falsehoods, such as the belief that pilgrims brought darts to America on the *Mayflower*. (Not true! Check out page 13 for the real scoop.) No one can accurately pinpoint the modern sport's precise origin, though it's accepted by pretty much all darts enthusiasts that it evolved from other target games, like archery and, later, "puff and dart" (learn more about that Victorian leisure activity on page 19).

Darts is a game for patrons of small local pubs and royalty alike (see page 53). Today, the professional leagues are filled with larger-than-life personalities (Bobby George, we're looking at you; see page 21) with colorful nicknames (see page 43) and unique musical selections that are always on target (see page 21).

Now the darts are in your hands, so to speak. Set up a board, grab some friends, and start throwing. Have fun!

The Dartboard Explained

The traditional British-style dartboard, also known as the London or clock board, is the standard target for most games of darts and is used in all major tournaments.

TRIPLES RING The inner scoring ring. A dart that lands here scores three times the number value of that segment.

OUTER BULL'S-EYE Worth 25 points. But in "double out" -01 games (see page 3), players cannot finish by hitting the outer bull's-eye.

SINGLE SCORING
Two segments on either side of the triples ring. A dart that lands here scores the number value of that segment.

INNER BULL'S-EYE
Worth 50 points. In -01 games, players can finish their game with the inner bull's-eye (which is essentially a double 25).

DOUBLES RING
The outer scoring ring. A dart that lands here scores twice the number value of that segment.

OUT OF PLAY A dart that lands in this area earns no point.

The Anatomy of a Dart

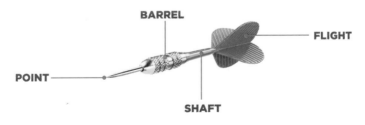

BARREL

FLIGHT

POINT

SHAFT

◎ *The Perfect Throw*

Whether you're playing with the mini darts included here or with the real thing, here are some throwing fundamentals you should know.

Grip a dart like you would a pencil. You should hold it between your thumb, index finger, and middle finger. Your thumb should sit naturally underneath the dart's center of gravity. Your fingers and thumb should apply firm, but light pressure—the dart should just fall out of your hand if you loosen up. No part of your body should move other than your throwing arm. Any other movements can result in inaccuracy.

The most common stance is known as "best foot forward." Imagine a line running from the center of the dartboard to the oche (the throwing line). Place your right foot (or left, if you're left-handed) directly on that line, with your toes pointing straight at the board. Shift more of your weight onto this foot to reduce the tendency to rock or lunge during your throw.

To throw, bring your arm up so that your dart is in a sighting position that's level with your right eye (or left, if

you're throwing with your left hand). Your elbow should be pointed at the dartboard and stay there throughout the entire throwing action. It serves as one of two pivots, the second being your wrist, which allows you to bring the dart back toward your ear without losing sight of it.

Keeping the rest of your body still, move your forearm forward (the only movement should be coming from your forearm and wrist). Your motion should form an arc, at the top of which you should release the dart with a light, fluid motion so it flies toward the target along the sight line. As in golf, follow-through is important for maintaining accuracy. Once you've released the dart, continue with the movement of the arc.

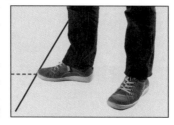

◉ *Darts Vocabulary*

If you're going play darts, you ought to know how to talk like a darts player. They lay claim to a fun and colorful language of their own, and with some practice you'll have it down. So make some flash cards and start brushing up on your darts vocabulary!

Bag o'nuts Scoring 45 points in a throw.

Bed-and-breakfast Hitting a 20, a 5, and a 1 in one turn, which is supposedly based on the price of a stay in an old English hostel: two shillings and six pence. Also known as a *classic*.

Beehives Cockney rhyming slang for "two 5s."

Bounce-out When your dart hits the wire frame and bounces off the dartboard. Also known as *wiring*.

Bread and lard Cockney rhyming slang for "hard" (as in a difficult shot).

Bubble The overused segment on a dartboard, usually around the triple 20, where the board has become loose and bubbles out.

Buck shot Any three darts that land off their intended target. Also known as *grape shot*.

Bust Scoring more points than needed to win a game.

Chalker The game's scorekeeper.

Closing out Hitting a number three times.

Cork The bull's-eye.

Cracked Hitting a single when you're aiming for a double.

Dead Hitting the exact score required.

Dead eye An American expression for hitting the double bull's-eye three times in a row.

Diddle for the middle A method for determining who goes first in a match—each player throws one dart, and whoever gets closest to the bull's-eye wins. Also known as *bulling-up*.

Double in/Double out Hitting a double to either start or end a game.

Fallout Hitting a scoring number that wasn't the one for which you were aiming.

Fat The area between the double and the triple ring; the largest portion of a number.

Father's boots An expression used to tell a person their foot is over the throw line and their throw won't count. Also known as *wet feet* and *moccasins* (in the U.S.).

Garden gates Cockney rhyming slang for two 8s or a score required of 88. Also known as *golden gates*.

Gertie Lee Cockney rhyming slang for 33.

Leg One game in a match.

Lipstick The triple 20. Also known as the *red bit*.

Madhouse Scoring on the double 1 for a win.

Married man's side The left side of the traditional dartboard, which has a concentration of higher numbers. It's encouraged to aim there for those looking to play it safe, allegedly a common trait of married men.

Mugs away A rule that allows the loser of the previous game to start the next game immediately, instead of diddling for the middle.

Nine-darter A perfect game of 501, achieved by throwing just nine darts.

Oche The line that you must stand behind to throw.

Off the island The non-scoring portion of a dartboard.

Pie Any of the numbered sections on the dartboard.

Right house, wrong bed Hitting a double or triple, but not hitting the number you intended.

Round of nine Hitting the triple 20, triple 19, and triple 18 at the start of a game of Cricket.

Shanghai Hitting a triple, double, and single of a number in the same turn.

Spider The wire assembly that forms the segments on a dartboard.

Split the 11 Throwing a dart between the two digits forming the number 11.

Swans of the lake Score of 22, because the two 2s look like swans.

Sunset Strip Scoring 77 points in a round.

Three in a bed When all three darts land on the same number during your turn.

Ton 80 180 points, the maximum possible score with three darts on a traditional dartboard, achieved by hitting the triple 20 with each dart. 100 points is considered a ton.

White horse The remarkable feat of hitting three triples in a round. It's a beautiful sight!

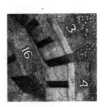

The Games

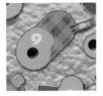

⦿ *501*

DOWN FOR THE COUNT

HOW TO PLAY

It's time to master the most popular darts game in the world. If you're in a tournament, whether professional or in a local darts league, odds are you're playing a game of 501. The rules couldn't be simpler. Each player starts with 501 points and subtracts from that score with every throw, with three throws per turn. Doubles count for double and triples count for triple. The outer bull's-eye counts for 25 and the inner bull's-eye is worth 50. To win, a player must get down to *exactly* zero. For example, if 5 points remain, only hitting a single 5 will earn you the win. Most games follow the "bust" rule, meaning if you hit a number higher than what's needed, you bust your score and it reverts to the score you had at the start of that turn.

You'll need a scoreboard (see page 7 for a good example). Each player has two columns. In the outer column, keep track of the number of points you earn in the turn. In the inner column, write down how many points you have left—sort of like balancing your checkbook!

You're going to want to finish the game in the fewest number of throws. A familiarity with the basic mathematics of the dartboard is essential to planning ahead and knowing what numbers and combinations of singles, doubles, and triples to use to win the game. As you start to get closer to zero, think about the numbers you'll have to hit to have that clean ending.

AIMING FOR PERFECTION

A perfect game of 501 is finishing with just nine darts. Professional darts player John Lowe made history on October 13, 1984, when he threw the first televised nine-dart finish during the MFI World Matchplay Championship in Slough, England. During his first two turns, he hit six triple 20s. When he was up again, he hit a triple 17 (51 points), a triple 18 (54 points), and a double 18 (36 points). This accomplishment earned him £102,000, approximately $165,000 at the time. (Little side note: Lowe couldn't collect his earnings for two years due to complex British tax laws, but that's another story.)

MAKE IT SIMPLER

Instead of counting down from 501 points, start at 301, a common variation of the game. In fact, 301 was the original version of the game—501 didn't become the standard until the world's first nationally organized darts tournament, the *News of the World* Darts Championship, began in 1927.

TAKE IT UP A NOTCH

When you're playing straight-in, you begin scoring with your very first throw. The game can be made more challenging if players have to double-in, meaning you do not begin scoring until you hit a double. This method can quickly eliminate any advantage a player may have from being the first person to throw. Players can also be required to double-out, which is required in most competitive play. In this case, you run the additional risk of busting if you don't land on the double, even if you hit the number you need. Try your hand at going out with the highest number of achievable points: 170. This score can be accomplished with two triple 20s and the bull's-eye (i.e., a double 25).

And if you're playing in teams, or just want a longer game, start at 701, or, for the hearty among us, even 1,001.

Why -01, Anyway?

Games of -01 originated in English alehouses, where the scoring was derived from the card game cribbage, in which players kept score by inserting a peg into a wooden cribbage board that had two sets of 60 holes on each side as well as an extra peg hole at each end. The darts scoring was recorded on the cribbage boards, with the game requiring players to go around the board five times (60 holes x 5 = 300) plus the extra hole. Even as players transitioned to using chalkboards to keep score, the -01 games remained.

2 ◎ *Finnish Darts*
SCANDINAVIAN STYLE

HOW TO PLAY

In Finland the game of darts is known as *tikka*, and our Finnish friends have their own unique board. Its design, as you can see, is very similar to that of a traditional archery target (like the one used in Cupid's Arrow on page 22). You'll sometimes find this board design on the backside of commercially available British-style boards, so you might already have one on your wall and simply not know it!

The object of Finnish darts is to earn the most points in five rounds, with five darts per round (instead of your usual three). Like American-style darts (see page 12), players share the same darts, but unlike American darts, the thrower is expected to retrieve the darts after their turn is over.

Create a scorecard that lists numbers 1 through 9 and the bull's-eye (which is worth 10 points), followed by columns for each of the players. In addition to tracking your overall score, you're going to want a tally of each number you hit, so put an X next to the number in your column each time you hit it. When a dart lands on a line between two numbers, it counts toward the higher number. The person with the highest score after five rounds is the winner, but in the event of a tie, the winner is the person who hit the most bull's-eyes. If the number of bull's-eyes is the same, the player who hit the 9 the most times wins, and so on.

MAKE IT SIMPLER

Finnish darts is a pretty straightforward game, but you can make it simpler by playing with just three darts, or by choosing a color and seeing how many times in a row you can hit that color before missing.

TAKE IT UP A NOTCH

A game of Finnish darts is generally shorter than British or American games since there are only five rounds. One way to mix it up is to play marathon-style, in which players take all 25 of their throws in a row. The only break players take is to retrieve the five darts. You might not think this will make much of a difference, but try maintaining your aim after you've thrown 16 or 17 darts. A break will start to sound mighty nice.

An alternative marathon style is having ten 5-round games, determining the winner based on who won the most number of games. Like the first variation, endurance is as important as accuracy. And as much as you love the game, "Is it my turn yet?" might soon become "Do I really have to go again?"

Finnish Prep Work

When playing a full size Finnish-style dartboard, your setup is going to be slightly different from that of a British-style board. The bull's-eye of the Finnish board should be 1.5 meters (approximately 5 feet) from the floor instead of the usual 5 feet 8 inches. And your throwing distance is a whopping 5 meters (a little less than 16 feet 5 inches) from the board, which is more than double the distance of the throwing line in British-style play. At that distance, if you're playing outdoors, you might have to start adjusting your aim to account for wind!

The setup and rules aren't the only differences between Finnish- and British-style darts. There's a cultural difference as well. The Finnish Darts Sports Association takes their matches very seriously, as it should. Any disturbance, such as shouting or touching, is strictly forbidden. According to the rules, players are allowed to file a written protest immediately after their own throw or the throw of another if they feel this rule has been violated. The competitions must be generally silent affairs; even unnecessary conversations with the referee are not allowed. In these professional competitions, men typically play in teams of five, whereas women, children, and seniors play in teams of three.

3 ◎ *Cricket*

IT'S CLOSE-OUT TIME!

HOW TO PLAY

The object of Cricket is to close out numbers 15 through 20, plus the bull, before your opponent does, while also earning points. (A quick reminder: A number is "closed out" when you hit it three times, or by hitting the triple or a double and a single.) To score points, keep hitting numbers that you've closed out but that your opponent has open. For example, if you close out 17 and then hit a double 17 before your opponent closes it, you earn 34 points. The inner and the outer bulls are worth 25 and 50 points, respectively. The game ends when one person closes out all the numbers and has the highest score. If you close out

everything first but your opponent is leading in points, you will need to hit their open numbers or bulls until you have a higher score. No player can score on a number (or the bull's) that has been closed out entirely.

You'll need to keep track of your score and the numbers you've closed out with a scoreboard. A chalkboard or piece of paper will do. Each player has two columns. Write the numbers 20 to 15 and the bulls down the center. (D, T, and 3B come into play if you decide to make the game a bit harder. See "Or Play This," below.) The inner column is where you keep track of the number of times you hit a number. If you hit it once, mark a slash next to it. The second time you hit it, make another slash to form an X. The third time, draw a circle around the X. Once it's closed out, you can keep track of the points you score on that particular number in the outer column.

MAKE IT SIMPLER

Try No-Score Cricket. Just as the name suggests, there's no scoring involved with this game. The object is solely to be the first person to close out all the numbers and the bull's.

◎ OR PLAY THIS: TACTICS

If you're looking for an additional challenge, try playing the version of Cricket known as Tactics or Wild Mouse. In this version, in addition to closing out 15 through 20, players must hit three doubles, three triples, and three bed shots (all three darts in the same number); these are represented on the scoreboard as D, T, and 3B, respectively. As with the numbers on the board, you can start scoring on these targets once you've hit them three times. Depending on your proficiency, you can play Slop Rules Tactics, where all doubles and triples on the board are in play, or Strict Tactics, where only doubles and triples from 15 to 20 count.

Keep in mind, one dart can't count for two different objectives. If you hit a triple 15 with a throw, you can count it toward three 15s or one of your triples, but not both. This game will take a bit longer than regular Cricket, but will go a long way in refining your accuracy.

A traditional darts scoreboard that can be used for Cricket and 501

The Name Game

Arguably the most popular darts game in the United States, Cricket has a vast array of nicknames and variations. It is known as Mickey Mouse, Horse and Carriage, Newfie, Chase, and, most appropriately, The Game. You can stretch the game out by playing from 12 to 20 instead of from 15. Try a game of Cut-Throat Cricket, in which players' points are awarded to their opponents' and the winner is the player with the fewest points. Or try your hand at Scram, which is played over two rounds. In the first round, one player tries to close out numbers while the other person scores, and in the second, they switch. The player with the highest number of points after the two rounds is the winner. However, don't expect to play a game anything like these if you're asked to play Cricket in the United Kingdom. The English game of Cricket comes with its own set of rules, derived from the outdoor ball-and-bat game.

4 ◎ *Shanghai*

SEIZE AN INSTANT WIN

HOW TO PLAY

Another classic darts game, Shanghai is played by shooting at numbers 1 to 20 on the board in sequential order—one number per round. It can be played with any number of people or teams. The object of the game is to score the highest number of points—the catch is that only hitting the number of the round will earn you those points.

Break out a chalkboard or a piece of paper and write the numbers 1 to 20 down the left side. Keep track of the points you score as you go from round to round. Hitting the double or the triple of the number will earn you a higher score. The highest score after the twentieth round wins . . . unless you "shanghai" your opponent for an instant win. A shanghai is achieved by hitting a single, a double, and a triple in a single round. If you achieve a shanghai and your opponent has not yet had a turn in that round, he or she is afforded the chance to get a shanghai as well. If your opponent makes it too, the game continues into the next round and once more the winner will be whoever has the highest score at the end of twenty rounds.

ELIMINATION MODE

When playing with three or more players, one way to keep people on their toes is by choosing certain rounds where everyone must score. So if round five is designated, each player must score at least once with their throws. Even if a player is leading in points after the first four rounds, missing in the fifth round will take them out of the game. Mark these rounds with an asterisk on the score sheet.

MAKE IT SIMPLER

If you're still honing your accuracy, feel free to shoot at the numbers out of order for twenty rounds, knowing you can only score on the first number you hit during that turn. You can still keep track on the same scoreboard, but hop around as you go from number to number. Also, you can designate a bull's-eye as the shanghai instead of having to throw a single, double, and triple in one round. Land on the bull's-eye once and the game is yours.

TAKE IT UP A NOTCH

Once you've trained yourself to achieve a shanghai with ease, make the game more challenging by requiring players to earn that shanghai in the proper order: a single, a double, and then a triple for it to count.

Classic Varieties

The traditional British-style dartboard is also known as the London or clock board. In the early 1900s, there were at least twenty regional variations in Great Britain. Here are four of the boards you might have seen in pubs throughout the country. Can you spot the difference?

Manchester Log-End Board

Yorkshire Board

East London Fives Board

Grimsby Board

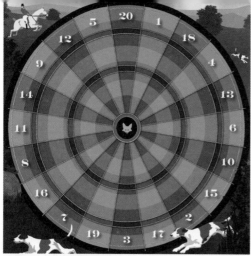

Fox Hunt

OUTFOX 'EM

HOW TO PLAY

A classic darts game that can be played on any board, Fox Hunt is a chase in which one player assumes the role of the fox and the other is the hound. The object of the game is for the fox to flee from the hound by traveling counter-clockwise around the board, starting at the top of the board with the number 20. To move forward from one number to the next, the fox must hit each number. Meanwhile, the hound is trailing behind, starting at number 18. Like the fox, the hound must hit each number in order to advance. Both players have three throws per turn to get to

the next number, but once it's reached, the next person is up.

Unlike other games, the two players have different objectives in order to win. The fox needs to make its way home by going all the way around the board. After it has returned to the 20 segment, it must aim for and hit its foxhole, aka the bull's-eye. Meanwhile, the hound needs only to catch up to the fox's number in order to win. If the fox wins, make a note of how many numbers behind the hound was. If the hound wins, note on which number it caught the fox. You'll need this information later, as the game isn't over just yet.

Now switch roles and play again to see if the new fox can make better progress than the original one did. If the new fox makes it back to the foxhole as well, the game's winner is determined by how far behind each hound was. The hound who was the fewest numbers behind is the winner. If the new fox is captured, the hound who captured it in the fewest number of segments is the winner.

It goes without saying that the fox and the hound are secretly best friends and no harm comes to either of them during this game. Anytime the hound catches the fox, of course he lets him go so they can play another round together!

MAKE IT SIMPLER

Why stop advancing at just one number? Depending on your aim, advance up to three numbers during your turn by continuing to throw. It'll make the chase a lot quicker, and could also put a lot of distance between the fox and the hound. If this game is going too quickly, feel free to add two or three extra laps around the board before getting to the foxhole.

TAKE IT UP A NOTCH

Increase the intensity of the hunt by requiring both the fox and the hound to hit both a single and a double of each number before being able to advance. Or if you want to make the fox sweat a little bit more, require it to hit a single and a double while the hound only needs to hit a double. And before the fox is home free, it must hit the foxhole three times, giving the hound ample opportunity to catch up. Once the first chase is over, as before, switch roles and go again. Happy hunting!

Hobbyists of Another Feather

As you might recall, the back "featherlike" portion of a dart is called the flight. Its purpose is to produce drag—preventing the rear of the dart from overtaking the point—as well as to increase stability to avoid wobbling.

Most flights today are made from thermo-sealed laminated polyester. Believe it or not, flights themselves are objects of desire among some collectors, who seek and acquire flights the way other hobbyists pursue coins, stamps, or comic books. These collectors are known as belopterophilists. That mouthful was coined by J. W. Clifton of the Queen's English Society in 1988. When you break it apart, it makes more sense: *Belos* means "dart," *ptero* means "flight," and *philist* means "collector." Now try saying it three times fast!

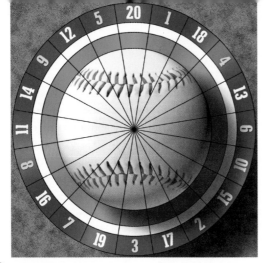

6 ◎ *American Darts*

BATTER UP!

HOW TO PLAY

Classic American Darts is based on the rules of baseball. The object is to get the highest score after nine consecutive innings. Each player gets three darts for each inning. During any given inning, you must hit the inning number every time you throw to be awarded points. The large white area is worth a single point, the red ring is worth 2, and the thin white ring is worth 3. And in an interesting change, the bull's-eye is actually worth zero, as is the blue ring, which is an out-of-bounds marker and not a scoring area. In any given inning, the highest score is 9, which is achievable by hitting the triple ring three times. If there's a tie, proceed with extra innings until a winner emerges.

In addition to the different board, American Darts comes with its own rules and etiquette. Unlike the English game, players share a single set of darts instead of having their own. And it is common practice for each player to leave the darts in the board for the next player to retrieve, allowing the next player to verify their opponent's score.

MAKE IT SIMPLER

To make the game a bit easier, open up the entire board for scoring and use each section's number as the point value. You'll still have to maintain accuracy to get the high points, but you'll no longer be limited to a thin sliver of the board each inning.

◎ OR PLAY THIS: STRIKEOUT

If you're looking for a more difficult take on American Darts, trying playing Strikeout. In this variation, each player's first throw assigns them a number for the game and that's the only number for which they'll be able to earn points. Obviously you'll want the 20, but don't fret if you're stuck with a low number; you can get 100 points each time you hit the bull's-eye. The person with the highest score after nine innings is the winner.

Though legend has it that the Pilgrims brought darts to America on the *Mayflower*, thorough research by darts experts Patrick Chaplin, Ph.D., and William Peek points to the game arriving much later in our nation's history. Peek's investigation led him to conclude that John Pearson, an English immigrant and tavern owner in Philadelphia, was the first person to make a dartboard in the U.S. in the early 1900s, despite the earliest darts-related patents not appearing until 1924. According to a 1952 *Philadelphia Evening Bulletin* article that Peek found, John Pearson fashioned his dartboard from a cross-section slab of a tree and put it up in his tavern. Pearson's son and grandson, Tom and Jack Tempest, would go on to form the Dartboard Equipment Company, also

The American-style board was first played around Philadelphia and in the coal regions of northeastern Pennsylvania. It is still found primarily in eastern states such as New York, New Jersey, Delaware, and Maryland.

known as DECO, a leader in the dartboard manufacturing business.

Throughout the years, Tom Tempest often clashed with Charles "Widdy" Widemeier Sr., founder of a rival dartboard business, the Widdy Company, over who was first to make American-style boards. To Widemeier's

credit, darts are sometimes called "widdies" in areas where the American-style game is played. There is also evidence that neither Widemeier nor Tempest can take responsibility, and instead that the honors may belong to the Apex Manufacturing Company. Once a manufacturer of wooden ladders, Apex turned to dartboards after World War I. In an article from *Sporting Goods Journal* believed to be from 1923, Apex is credited with introducing a "new kind of darts game." This article remains the earliest documented reference to the American-style board, which retained its place as the country's predominant type of board until the 1960s, when the British-style board began to grow in popularity outside of its native country.

7 ◎ *Mulligan*
CLOSE-OUT FACE-OFF

HOW TO PLAY

The game of Mulligan requires equal parts skill and patience. The rules are fairly straightforward: Close out six randomly chosen numbers plus the bull's-eye before your opponent. To close out a number, you must hit it three times. The doubles ring counts for double and the triples for triple. The random numbers can be selected any way you please, such as via a pregame round of throwing at the board with your opposite hand. Depending on the number of players, you may share some of the same numbers.

You'll want to keep track of your numbers on a scoreboard similar to the one used for Cricket (see page 7). Each player has two columns. In the left column, write the numbers you've chosen. In the right column, track your progress. Just as in Cricket, if you hit a number once, mark a slash next to it. The second time you hit it, make another slash to form an X. The third and final time, draw a circle around the X.

You're not going to master this game overnight, but that shouldn't stop you from trying it out and seeing how you do.

Who Arranged Those Numbers?

A DARTBOARD WITH THE STANDARD twenty segments has over 121 quadrillion possible numerical arrangements. Remarkably, this board is nearly mathematically perfect in penalizing poor shots, as high numbers are flanked by low numbers on both sides.

Carpenter Brian Gamlin is generally credited with creating this sequence in 1896, though historians have been unable to uncover any official record of him. Another man, Thomas William Buckle, might have been the board's inventor. In 1913, he is believed to have adapted the twelve-segment Fives board (see page 9) into the twenty-segment board we know today.

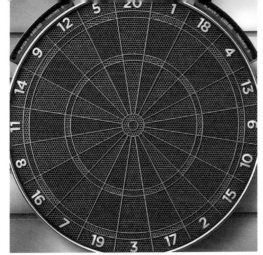

8 ⊚ Over/Under
WHAT ARE THE ODDS?

HOW TO PLAY

Place your bets now. What are the odds that you can score over 42 or under 21 points each turn with three throws? In this game, you have to or you'll get a strike. Keep in mind, the doubles ring counts for double and the triples ring counts for triple, so your score can multiply very quickly if your aim is even slightly off. If you're trailing behind, start shooting for the bull's-eye. Each time you hit it, your opponent gets a strike. Don't abuse this opportunity, as it would be a quick way to turn your opponent into a sworn enemy (and it is poor sportsmanship). After ten rounds, the player with the fewest strikes is the winner.

A Safe Bet

IN 1908, ENGLISH LAW PROHIBITED BETTING ON games of chance in establishments that sold alcohol. Betting on games of skill, however, was permitted. Jim Garside, landlord of the Adelphi Inn, a beerhouse in Leeds, was brought before the court on charges of violating this law because he allowed betting on darts matches. Garside asserted that darts was in fact a game of skill and invited William "Bigfoot" Anakin, local darts champ, to back up his claim.

After this point, accounts of what occurred in the courtroom vary. Some believe that Anakin arrived with his own Yorkshire dartboard and showed off his ability by throwing three darts into the single 20 segment. A clerk of the court was then asked to throw three darts, only one of which actually hit and stuck in the board. Anakin went again, this time throwing three darts into the double ring. Other accounts say he threw three triple 20s, equally impressive but also impossible, since Yorkshire boards had no triple ring. According to Anakin's grandson, he hit a series of numbers that were called out to him, which was enough for the court magistrates to deem darts a game of skill, not chance. Regardless of what actually went down, the charges against Garside were dismissed.

9 ◎ Shooting Hoops

GOT GAME?

HOW TO PLAY

Unwind after a long day by shooting hoops with a friend—no need for a basketball court. To land those 3-pointers, your dart must land exactly within the hoop. For a 2-point shot, aim for the red box above the net (also known as the shooter's square, if you want to get technical). Each player has three throws to score per turn, though some extra opportunities will arise over the course of the game. An offensive rebound or a personal foul will earn you an extra throw. And if you luck out hitting the bank shot, you earn an extra point. You run the risk of losing your turn if you hit a technical foul, defensive rebound, or a blocked shot, so be careful. An air ball will also result in losing your turn, not to mention some heckling from your opponent. The person with the highest score after fifteen minutes is the winner.

MAKE IT SIMPLER

You've got a basketball hoop, so of course you're going to want to play H-O-R-S-E every so often. You know the rules: Take turns calling your shots, either a 3-pointer in the net, a 2-pointer off the backboard, or a bank shot for 1 point if you're feeling up to it. Stand anywhere you want in relation to the board (as long as your feet are a minimum of 5 feet away). If you land the shot you called, your opponent has to make the same one, from the same spot, or they get a letter. Keep taking turns and calling shots until someone has spelled H-O-R-S-E and the game is over.

TAKE IT UP A NOTCH

In a real game of one-on-one, the player on defense doesn't just stand around while the other person shoots. So in this game, while the offensive player throws for points, the defensive player can try to prevent him from scoring. Find a stance that's comfortable for both players, where each can see the board and throw comfortably, alternating dart for dart. While the offense aims for the hoop or shooter's square, the defense needs to aim for a technical foul, blocked shot, or a defensive rebound. If the offensive player lands a 2- or 3-point shot but the defensive player hits one of his targets, the round goes to the defense. However, if the offensive player hits a personal foul or offensive rebound, the round goes to the offense and that player gets to take the next shot unobstructed. Alternate between offense and defense with each round, and see who can score the most points in a twenty-minute game.

Day Jobs

Part of the appeal of darts over the years is its "everyman" aspect. *Anyone* could be a professional player. With that in mind, take a look at some of the former and/ or current careers of these darts greats.

Eric Bristow (*above*) —Proofreader for an advertising agency

Stacy Bromberg— Private investigator

Bobby George— Bouncer, window cleaner, and tunnel digger, among other gigs

Trina Gulliver (*below*)—Carpenter and teacher

Terry Jenkins— Antiques dealer

John Lowe— Carpenter

Wayne Mardle (*above*)—Accountant

Andy Smith—Tree surgeon

Co Stompé—Tram (streetcar) driver

Phil Taylor (*below*)— Maker of ceramic toilet chains and beer pump handles

Robert Wagner— Bodybuilder

Mark Webster— Plumber

Pyramid Power

THROW LIKE AN EGYPTIAN

HOW TO PLAY

A pyramid took twenty to thirty years and thousands of hours of labor to build, according to most estimates. How long is it going to take you to climb one? You'll be racing an opponent to the top, and of course you want to be the first one to get there. Reach the pyramid's apex by hitting every number from 1 to 24 in order, with three throws per turn. So if you're at the top of the game, it would only take eight full turns to accomplish it. If you fall behind, you can turn to the Eye of Horus, which is hovering above the pyramid. The Eye is an ancient Egyptian symbol of protection and good health, and hitting it allows you to jump up a level. For example, if you're at the number 7, you can skip to 13. But as you ascend the heights of the pyramid, you must also be mindful of Anubis, the god of death, who hovers on all sides. Hitting the god of death will drop you down a level. Once you've reached the top, celebrate your accomplishment by hitting the Eye of Horus three times. The first person to do so is the winner!

MAKE IT SIMPLER

If this is your first expedition, it helps to bring some extra equipment. Try reaching the top with six throws per turn instead of three. Worry not about Anubis and just focus on getting to the top, where the Eye of Horus will be waiting, and just one hit will be required to win the game.

TAKE IT UP A NOTCH

Experienced adventurers will probably be looking for more of a challenge, and this is just the ticket. To truly understand the majesty of the Egyptian pyramids, one must appreciate the mathematical precision it took to construct them, stone by stone. To that end, with three throws per turn, in order to ascend from level to level, each player must earn a score equal or greater to a value of a block on the next level. So if you want to get to the number 7 block, you must score at least 7 from the first level. You can only advance one level at a time, so even though hitting the 6 block three times is impressive, it's not going to get you higher than the 12 block. The first person to reach the top and hit the Eye of Horus three times is the winner. As before, Anubis is nearby at all times—avoid him or risk a fall to the bottom of the pyramid.

The Darts Family Tree

There comes a point in every parent's life when his or her child innocently asks, "Where do darts come from?" It's helpful to have an answer at the ready. One of darts' earliest ancestors was a sixteenth-century game called "puff and dart," first documented in Joseph Strutt's *Sports and Pastimes of the People of England* in 1801. This game entailed blowing a small dart through a pipe at a concentric, miniature archery target. Whoever earned the highest score with three puffed darts was the winner. The game was popular both in pubs and upper-class Victorian homes, where it was known as "drawing room archery."

If you're wondering what happened to this game, look no further than the British medical journal *The Lancet*. In 1883, they described the dangers of "puff and dart": A high number of injuries were sustained by people sucking on the pipe instead of blowing, inhaling the small darts into their stomachs and lungs. Doctors condemned the game as unsafe and potentially fatal. Manufacturers developed a safer puff dart, but the damage was done. In comparison, darts thrown by hand seemed positively harmless.

"Puff and dart" was played in pubs and parlors alike.

11 ◎ Stonehenge Calling

RITUAL ON THE ROCKS

HOW TO PLAY

Unlock the mysteries of Stonehenge with a ritual that will leave only one soul standing. Start off the game by shooting for the altar. The first person to hit it begins the game by calling a numbered stone and then aiming for it with a dart. A turn ends with the successful shot or after three throws. If the shooter hits their called number, the second player must attempt the same shot with three tries, thus completing the ritual. If he misses, he gets a strike and the next player gets to call the shots. If the first player is on a streak and keeps making his shots, the second player can opt to turn the tables by hitting the Heel Stone, which earns them the chance to start calling shots. This move is risky as it invites the possibility of getting a quick extra strike. The first person to receive ten strikes loses the chance to learn Stonehenge's secrets. However, you can remove a strike by hitting the 11 stone twice in a row. You can only remove up to three strikes per game.

MAKE IT SIMPLER

Play for points instead of strikes. This way, no one loses the game for too many misses. The first player still picks the stone, and both players shoot for that stone, but if you hit it more than once during each turn, add up the points. In this game, both the Heel Stone and the Altar count for 25 points. The highest score after ten rounds is the winner.

TAKE IT UP A NOTCH

Close out as many stones as you can after hitting each one three times over the course of the game. You'll need to keep track of which stones you've hit each turn. Once a stone is closed out, it can no longer be used in play. After all the stones and the Heel are closed out, whoever closed out the most wins. In the event of a tie, take turns aiming for the altar, one throw per turn, until someone misses.

Grand Entrances

Speaking of rituals, there's one that professional darts players delight in: They all have their own walk-on song at the start of a game, which they use to set the tone for the match. The song can be playful, boastful, intimidating, or simply fitting for the occasion. Here's just a sampling of walk-on songs from some of the greats. Together, they would make one heck of a playlist! See if this lineup inspires you to imagine what your walk-on song would be.

Stacy Bromberg—"American Girl" by Tom Petty

Alan Warriner-Little—"Cold as Ice" by Foreigner

Eric Bristow—"Crazy Nights" by KISS

Gary Robson—"Don't Worry, Be Happy" by Bobby McFerrin

Andy Smith—"Eat It" by "Weird Al" Yankovic

Raymond van Barneveld—"Eye of the Tiger" by Survivor

Phil Taylor—"Fanfare for the Common Man" by Aaron Copland

Wayne "Hawaii 501" Mardle—"Hawaii Five-O" by the Ventures

Denis Ovens—"The Heat Is On" by Glenn Frey

Martin Adams—"Hungry Like the Wolf" by Duran Duran

John Part—"The Imperial March (Darth Vader's Theme)" by John Williams

Gary Anderson—"Jump Around" by House of Pain

Jamie Caven—"Lust for Life" by Iggy Pop

Bob Anderson—"Rhinestone Cowboy" by Glen Campbell

Rod Harrington—"Sharp Dressed Man" by ZZ Top

Andy Hamilton—"U Can't Touch This" by MC Hammer

Terry Jenkins—"Wooly Bully" by Sam the Sham & The Pharaohs

Bobby George—"We Are the Champions" by Queen

The legendary Bobby George perfected the art of showmanship, often arriving to his matches wearing a cape, a crown, plenty of gold jewelry, and a candelabra in his mouth.

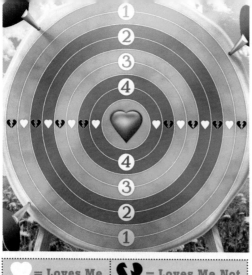

♥ = Loves Me   💔 = Loves Me Not

Cupid's Arrow

LOVE HURTS . . .

HOW TO PLAY

Even Cupid, that cherubic master archer, had to perfect his accuracy by shooting at a target every once in a while. Why don't you try his one-of-a-kind target board? Here's a chance to use your skill to discover if your sweetie truly only has eyes for you. With six darts per turn, start by hitting the heart-shaped bull's-eye, the symbol of your own fluttering heart. From there, with your remaining darts (whether it is one dart or five darts), shoot for the Loves Me rings to earn points. As for those Loves Me Not rings, they're worth negative points, which you'll have to deduct from your score. The player with the most points after ten rounds wins their heart's desire.

MAKE IT SIMPLER

You can't hurry love, but you can start scoring points sooner with this easier variation. With three throws per turn, skip aiming for the bull's-eye and try to earn points with every throw you take. Hitting the same number three times in one turn will double your overall score for that turn, so if you hit the 4 ring three times, your score will be 24 instead of 12. The heart-shaped bull's-eye is worth 5 points, but the pink ring that surrounds it is worth -5. Don't let that dissuade you from trying to reach it. Love is worth the risk sometimes.

TAKE IT UP A NOTCH

Now's your chance to prove that love is blind. Take your throws with your eyes closed and let your heart guide the darts to their destination. Now, now, we don't want to hear, "That's ridiculous! Irrational, too!" Well, friend, so is love, so take a leap of faith and see what happens with three throws per turn. The heart-shaped bull's-eye is worth 50 points. The "Loves Me Not" rings still have negative point values, but if you miss the board entirely, your score stays the same for that round. The person with the highest score after the tenth round wins the game. (Now, before you close your eyes, please read the following disclaimer out loud: The authors and the publisher do not recommend playing this game with actual darts, as throwing sharp objects with your eyes closed is extremely unsafe unless you're a trained circus performer. Thank you. And may your throwing arm lead you to true love!)

Misplaced Affection

King Henry VIII may or may not have played darts, but he was quite the sportsman.

Sorting through the mythology built up around darts is nearly as interesting as the game itself. For example, many believe the game of darts dates back to the sixteenth century and was a beloved pastime of King Henry VIII, thanks to documented accounts of the king receiving an ornate set of darts from his wife, Anne Boleyn, at a New Year's gift exchange in 1532. Historians still disagree about what those darts actually were. As amusing as it is to imagine King Henry playing 501, the truth is that darts as we know it today would bear little resemblance to any game played then. The "darts" that Anne gave her husband were most likely hunting spears, as the king had a penchant for hunting wild boar. In case you're wondering, King Henry VIII gave Anne a roomful of tapestries that year. It's almost hard to believe that just four years later, he'd be ordering her execution. Perhaps not all love is meant to be.

13 ◎ *Pinball*

BECOME A PINBALL WIZARD

HOW TO PLAY

Rack up the highest number of points in ten rounds of pinball. Just like real pinball, each turn lasts as long as you can stay in play. You continue to score points throw after throw, until you miss a target. If you hit a target with a negative point value, subtract those points from your score, but you're still in play. And each time you achieve nine throws in a turn, regardless of point value, add 100 bonus points to your score. Aim with care. Once you miss a target, your turn is over. After the tenth round, count up the points and see who is the true pinball wizard.

MAKE IT SIMPLER

Enjoy the possibility of getting outrageously high scores by attempting to repeatedly hit targets of the same point values. After you've hit a point value three or more consecutive times in a turn, multiply your final score on that value by the number of times you've hit it. For example, if you scored 50 points four times in a row, multiple that total of 200 by 4, for a new total of 800! (Note: You don't have to shoot at the same 50-point target each time. It can be *any* 50-point target on the board.) If you finish up your ten-round game with a score in the 1,000s, that's an accomplishment that might inspire you to make an all-time-high scoreboard to write in your achievements. Some things are worth bragging about, after all.

TAKE IT UP A NOTCH

No game of pinball begins until you launch the ball into play, so to start your turns, shoot for the ball in the bottom-right corner—you have up to three shots to hit it. If you miss it all three times, that's it, no points for your turn! Once you've launched the ball, keep going for as long as you can . . . but you're only going to score on a target if you've hit it three times in a row. Keep throwing until you miss scoring on a target. As above, triple, quadruple, quintuple, or even sextuple your score with a streak of the same point value or get the 100-point bonus for a streak of scoring nine times in a turn. Scoring nine times means 27 direct hits. It may seem impossible, but that's what makes this a game for pros.

For the Record

A number of darts records have made it into the *Guinness World Records*. Here are a few, in case you're ambitious and want to try to beat one.

The **farthest distance** from which a bull's-eye was thrown in darts: Malcolm Woolaston hit the bull's-eye from 5 meters (16 feet 4 inches) in Bournemouth, U.K., on January 12, 2011. It took him nearly eight minutes of throwing to hit it.

The **first nine-dart finish** in a World Championship match: Paul Lim finished with nine darts against Jack McKenna at Lakeside, Frimley Green, U.K., on January 9, 1990.

The **most maximums** scored by an individual darter in a Professional Darts Corporation World Championship: 180 is the highest achievable score, accomplished by hitting the triple 20 three times in a turn. Adrian Lewis threw 60 maximums at Alexandra Palace, London, on January 3, 2011.

The **most World Championship titles** won:

Paul Lim had a record-breaking finish in 1990.

Phil Taylor won fifteen World Championships, two with the World Darts Organization in 1990 and 1992, and thirteen with the Professional Darts Corporation in 1995–2002, 2004–2006, and 2009–2010.

The **youngest player** to participate in a competitive darts tournament: Nick Stoekenbroek was just twelve years old when he played the Dutch Open, Veldhoven, Netherlands, which ran from February 5–7, 2002.

The **oldest competitive darts player**: Candy Miller (born October 21, 1920) began playing in 1966 and still throws with her league twice a week, on Tuesday and Thursday nights.

you hit the 8 ball anytime *before* clearing all your balls, you lose the game automatically.

If you and your friends want to make the game a bit more challenging, bring the cue ball into play, just as you would in an actual game of pool: To sink a shot, you have to first hit the cue, then one of your balls, and finally a pocket. With only three throws per turn, not a single dart can be wasted.

14 ◎ *Pool*

THIRD DART, CORNER POCKET

HOW TO PLAY

Like darts, pool is another staple game in pubs and recreation rooms the world over. It typically requires a lot more physical space than darts . . . until now. We've shrunk down the table, but the rules remain the same in this billiards game. The object, of course, is to be the first player to get all your balls off the table. In order to do so, you must first hit a ball and then hit the pocket you want it to go in. You've got three throws per turn to sink the shot. One player or team takes the solid balls, the other takes the stripes. After you've sunk all your balls, aim for the 8 ball. Once you've sent it into one of the pockets, the game is yours! But if

---

Flipping Over Darts

INFAMOUS GANG LEADER AND CRIMINAL Isaac Bogard, who lived in London's East End in the early twentieth century, made a unique contribution to the history of darts. He owned a Jack Russell terrier-type mutt named Pipey, who was trained to stand on his hind legs and do a backflip anytime Bogard scored a bull's-eye. The audience was encouraged to reward the pooch by placing loose change in a bowler hat at Pipey's feet. The fact that Bogard had time to train the dog, play darts, and run a violent gang is impressive in and of itself. He later went into the service during World War I and emerged a hero, and was even awarded the British Army's Military Medal.

or diagonally. To close out a number, you must hit it three times. You don't have to close out one number before moving on to the next, so be sure to keep track of the hits you've made with a scorecard. And both players can close out the same numbers, so there's no need to fight over spots.

Just as you would in an actual game of bingo, take advantage of the Free circle. To amp up the challenge, you can require players to close out the Free circle in order to take advantage of it.

A fun variation is to have the first thrower in each round call out the letter and number. If they make the shot, then the other players also have to shoot for it. Each person who makes it can check that letter/number off their scorecard. In this version, hitting the number once is enough to make it yours. Otherwise, you'd probably be playing for hours.

Bingo
WILD CARD

HOW TO PLAY

It's going to take more than luck and random numbers to win this game of bingo. Be the first person to close out five numbers in a row—vertically, horizontally,

---

Made in America

BEFORE SYNTHETIC MATERIALS became the norm, paper was used to make the flights for darts. And despite the game's origins in England, it was actually an American who first invented paper flights—a gentleman by the name of Nathan P. McKenney from Dixon, Illinois. He filed the patent in March 1898, and it was approved the following November. Before McKenney's invention, flights were made from feathers. The two types of flights coexisted for the next few decades until plastic, nylon, and polyester flights became the standard. These days, it's rare to see paper flights, but McKenney's invention was a critical step in the evolution of the dart.

16 ◎ # The End of the World

KEEP DOOMSDAY AT BAY

HOW TO PLAY

Remember how the world was slated to end on December 21, 2012, because the Mayan calendar supposedly predicted it? Luckily, it didn't happen, and we still have this pretty awesome Mayan calendar, which makes a great dartboard! Try your own countdown by targeting every glyph (i.e., those colorful little pictures) on the board with three throws per turn. The twenty glyphs on the outer ring need to be hit only once. The six glyphs on the inner ring need to be hit twice, and the center glyph, which looks like it's mocking us for

believing that "end of the world" tomfoolery, needs to be hit three times. The first person to accomplish this wins . . . if they can manage to do it in twenty minutes or less. This game is a countdown, after all. If not, turn back the clock and start again.

MAKE IT SIMPLER

So we beat the clock when the world didn't end. Why rush anything anymore? Let's swap out twenty minutes for twenty rounds, trying to score the highest score with three throws per turn. The center glyph, an easy target compared to most bull's-eyes, is worth 5 points. The inner ring of glyphs is worth 10. Those tiny glyphs in the outer ring are worth 25. All the spaces in between? They'll cost you 5 points. And since we can't have this game be *too* easy, close out glyphs so your opponent cannot score on them. You can close one out by hitting it three times in a turn. If you're feeling feisty, take out the center glyph in your first turn, scoring 15 points, thereby making your opponent rely on the harder-to-hit glyphs for the rest of the game!

TAKE IT UP A NOTCH

Make the game more challenging by going from the outer ring inward or the center ring outward, but in order, one glyph at a time. Aim for the outer glyphs clockwise, starting from the top. And then to change it up, hit the inner ring's glyphs twice, now going counter-clockwise. Think you can still do it in twenty minutes? If so, then try for fifteen. You've got all the time in the world. It's not going anywhere, after all!

The Dartboard Begins

When the sport began to develop in the late nineteenth century, dartboards were typically made from elm wood, with the numbers and segments painstakingly painted on. These boards needed to be soaked overnight after being used to allow the holes made by the darts to close up, and to keep them from being too hard and/or splitting. As the twentieth century rolled in, boards made of clay became popular, but they too had faults—they needed to be rolled flat occasionally and they gave off an unpleasant smell. Along came Ted Leggatt, an English chemist who invented odorless clay, appropriately called Nodor (i.e., "No Odor"). In addition to the clay boards, his company, also named Nodor, produced elm boards, but the real innovation was still to come.

Meet the sisal plant, a dartboard in the making.

Leggatt teamed with pub owner Frank Dabbs to develop a new kind of a board, made from short pieces of rope that had been laced vertically and bound. "The Original Bristle" board debuted in 1935. One of its key features was that the holes created by the darts closed up immediately after the darts were removed. The fiber used to make these boards came from the sisal plant, which was and is cultivated in only a few countries, including Brazil, Tanzania, and China. To this day, the best dartboards are made from sisal.

Labels on image:
7 CINTEOTL
4 MIXCOATL
3 OMETEOTL
8 CHANTICO
9 ATLATONAN
5 IXTLILTON
2 TETEOINNAN
1 XILONEN
6 EHECATL

17 ◎ Trip to the Stars
ONE SMALL STEP FOR DARTS

HOW TO PLAY

You're in luck—thanks to this game, you can play darts in a zero-gravity environment. You have stumbled upon a remarkable new solar system containing nine planets with conditions similar to those on Earth—perhaps one of them can sustain life. Now is your chance to explore and lay claim to the planets! In order to claim a planet, you must hit it three times in a single turn, with just three throws per turn. And to claim the more distant inner planets (7, 8, and 9), you must first reach them, traveling from the outer planets inward, one dart at a time. So, if you want to claim Atlatonan, you first have to land on every preceding planet, starting with Xilonen. The first person to safely claim the majority of the planets is the winner. "Safely" is the operative word here. Space travel is hardly without its danger. Accidently hitting the transmission satellite that's orbiting above Xilonen will cost you a turn; it'll take that long to repair. And the planets orbit a burning-hot sun just like ours, so if you miss your targeted planets and land there, it's game over. Safe travels, space explorer!

MAKE IT SIMPLER

Leave the conquering to the space tyrants. You're on a mission of peace and just want to experience these new worlds so you'll have something to tell your grandchildren. To take this tour of the solar system, hop from planet to planet with three throws per turn, landing on each planet in numerical order, from 1 (Xilonen) to 9 (Atlatonan), and then make your way back out to report what you've discovered. The first player to return to Xilonen is the winner.

TAKE IT UP A NOTCH

Visiting other planets is all well and good, but claiming them in your name is even better. But planting your flag takes persistence. In order to declare your rightful ownership of a planet, you must hit it the number of times indicated by its location in the solar system (have a scorecard handy to keep track of your hits). So Xilonen can be yours with just one direct hit. Chantico, however, will require eight hits, and Atlatonan will require nine. You have three throws per turn. The winner of the game is the first person to claim five planets, including at least two of the three closest to the sun. There's no automatic win if your opponent crashes into the sun; you still have to be the first to claim five planets.

The Silver Comet Takes Flight

Prior to 1937, darts were typically sold loose and in varied weights and designs. That all changed when Hungarian salesman Frank Lowy introduced the "Silver Comet" dart, drawing from his time working as an apprentice engineer and in a patent office. Whereas darts had previously been wooden or brass, Lowy designed an all-metal, chromium-plated dart with a small, streamlined screw-on cap. What started with a £6 investment (approximately $9 in U.S. currency back then, or $150 today) turned into the world's leading manufacturer of darts equipment and accessories: Unicorn Darts.

The revolutionary Silver Comet dart

In addition to packaging his revolutionary darts in sets of three, he marketed them to sporting goods stores instead of hardware stores and other venues where darts were previously sold. During the first year, an astounding 170,000 sets were sold. Lowy also led the way in marketing plastic dart flights, which were previously made from feathers or paper, and was one of the first to export darts on a large scale.

Lowy passed away in 1969, but in 1983, he was posthumously inducted into the National Sporting Goods Association's Sporting Goods Industry Hall of Fame for his contributions to the industry.

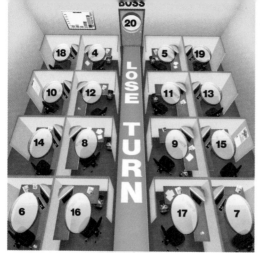

Office Wars

CLIMB THE CORPORATE LADDER

HOW TO PLAY

Here's a game about getting ahead in a cutthroat corporate world to play with your office buddies. The object is to stay one step ahead of your colleagues, otherwise known as the competition, at all times. The first player begins by throwing three darts and adding up his or her score. The next player now has to beat that score with three throws of their own. If the second player can't beat the first player's score, or if there is a tie, they receive a warning. After five warnings, you're canned.

Be careful not to be caught lingering in the aisle at any point during the game. If one of your throws lands there, you'll lose your turn. Now, I know what you're thinking—the first thrower gets off easy and doesn't have to worry about warnings. Not true! Switch the throwing order with each new round, giving each player the opportunity to throw first. And if you want to guarantee a warning for your opponent, go for the 9 to 5 special, hitting the numbers 9, 5, and then a knock on the boss's door for the 20. It's worth double points, making it the highest combination in play. Now, get to work!

MAKE IT SIMPLER

Some people know what they want to do with their lives from a very young age. Others have to move around and try different jobs until they find the right fit. Luckily, you're in an office that encourages you to find yourself. Take advantage of that by trying out every desk the office has to offer. With three throws per turn, be the first person to hit all of the cubicles. Start with the smallest number and work your way up through the office. Check each one off a scorecard as you move around.

No game would be complete without sitting in the boss's chair as well, so after you've hit all sixteen cubicles, start aiming for the number 20 on the boss's door. You'll have to knock—you guessed it—three times to gain entrance.

TAKE IT UP A NOTCH

If you really want to be the boss one day, you not only need to be able to do what your coworkers can do, you also have to motivate them to do better. It's called leadership, and you need to show your colleagues you have it in you. Once again, take turns, having one person shoot and the next person match it. But keep upping the ante with every round.

If the top score from the first round was 37, then the first shooter of the next round needs to get at least a 38 or they'll earn a warning themselves. A game like this one could lead to the players shooting for triple 20s every round—not that there's anything wrong with that. If you regularly hit lofty goals like these, you just might be in for an end-of-year bonus.

Playing by the Rules

According to the World Darts Federation:

• The longest time a player may be allowed between shooting individual darts is three minutes, which is generally only needed to replace or repair a dart.

• Though professional darts players do not wear uniforms, there is a dress code. All players must wear black trousers and shoes. Shirts may be any color, but must not feature anything that can be deemed offensive.

A gentlemanly finish to a match at the 2012 Ladbrokes.com World Darts Championship

• A player is allowed only six practice darts before commencing a match.

• The maximum allowable weight and length for a dart is 1.756 ounces and 12 inches, respectively.

Other rules and regulations vary across the globe, but one tradition seems to cross all borders— a hearty handshake before and after each match.

19 ◎ Passing Time
NOT A MINUTE TO WASTE

HOW TO PLAY

What we would've given to make the clock move a little bit faster during many long days at work or school. Now is your chance to speed up time by hitting every number on the board three times each, in consecutive order. Start with 9 o'clock, when your work day begins, and go around clockwise. When it's your turn, keep throwing until you miss. When you go again, you get to begin where you left off. Hitting the bull's-eye in the center allows you to either jump ahead a number or make your opponent fall back one hour; it's your call. Use the opportunity wisely, because your challenger can just as easily use it on you. The first person to make it all the way around the clock is . . . almost the winner. You can't call it quits and fully unwind until you've stopped the clock by landing three darts on the bull's-eye and then you can call it a night!

MAKE IT SIMPLER

Grab a piece of paper or whatever you're using to keep score, and write down numbers 1 through 12 on the left side. This game has twelve rounds, and in each one, you can only earn points on a single number, with three throws per turn. Points earned correlate to the number on the clock. So in round 1, shoot for the 1 o'clock hour. Score 1 point per hit, but if you land all three, double your score (that's 3 points times 2, or 6 points). The early rounds will be very low scoring, so don't get dissuaded if you're behind. Treat it as warm-up. You can turn it all around with some of the higher numbers—landing all three darts at 11 o'clock will net you 66 points! The person with the highest score at midnight wins the game.

TAKE IT UP A NOTCH

You're going to need a stopwatch in order to play this speed round. The rules are similar to the preceding version; you'll be aiming for one number at a time, only scoring off one number a round. But now you're allowed to throw as many darts as you can, provided you throw them in one minute per round. The double-score bonus remains in place as long as every throw lands on the number. For example, if you managed to throw 25 darts at 1 o'clock and every single one made it, your score for the round is 50. But if you throw 25 darts and only 24 made it in the one minute, sorry, your score remains 24 (which is still darn impressive). Whoever has the highest score at the end is the winner.

Time to Impress

Darts maestro Jim Pike

Here's an incredible record you can try to duplicate—or beat! In 1937, the legendary Jim Pike went around the entire dartboard, throwing at the doubles for every number and retrieving his own darts, in the lightning-quick time of three minutes, thirty seconds. And he stood 9 feet away from the board, unlike today's widely accepted distance of 7 feet 9¼ inches.

Pike was one of the most proficient players of his time, and his marksmanship was uncanny. He was said to be able to throw a dart that could knock a cigarette from your mouth and pin it to a double on the board. (You'd hate to be the person he practiced that trick on.)

In addition to being such a showman, Pike was also quite the do-gooder. During World War II, he captained the *News of the World* Team of Darts Champions, a group that raised money for the Red Cross and other wartime charities. His team raised hundreds of thousands of British pounds, more than any other sport during the war effort.

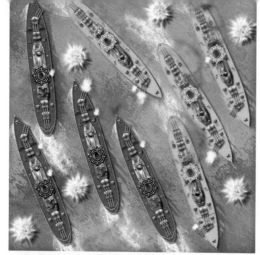

20 ◎ *Battle at Sea*

SINK OR SWIM

HOW TO PLAY

So much for a calm, peaceful day at sea. You're a petty officer third class aboard the USS *Hawaii*. Your fleet is on its way home for shore leave when all of a sudden, the ocean is filled with rogue battleships. All the gunmen have been incapacitated after eating some bad shellfish, and it's come down to just you to save the entire fleet by manning the gun turrets and sending your enemy's ships down to Davy Jones's Locker. And, believe it or not, your opponent is in the same boat (metaphorically speaking!), so you both need to choose a color and start firing away at each other.

In order to sink a battleship, you have to either hit it five times or land a direct hit on its conning tower, conveniently marked with a bull's-eye. You can focus on one enemy battleship at a time or jump around from ship to ship. Just make sure to keep track of your hits to avoid any confusion (or protests from your opponent). Each player gets three throws per round, and you can pick up where you left off when it's your turn again. In the heat of battle, it's always possible to get confused and cause some friendly fire by hitting one of your own ships. If this happens, you lose your turn. Watch out: If you go three rounds without sinking a battleship, you've given your enemy enough time to target you and retaliate. In other words, game over for you. Otherwise, the first person to sink all four of their opponent's ships goes home the hero.

MAKE IT SIMPLER

Imagine this battle is a video game simulation and you have unlimited ammunition. For each turn, keep throwing until you miss, whether it's three darts or twenty. Be sure to keep track of your number of throws each round. The player who goes first in each round has a bit of an advantage, so to balance things out, the second player will get the opportunity to match or beat the number of throws it took for the first player to sink all of their targets.

TAKE IT UP A NOTCH

Elimination mode will test your endurance and keep you on your toes. As in the simplified variation, you have unlimited ammunition, but your enemy now has unlimited ships. So even if you sink one ship, another is in its place almost instantly. Each player is allowed to keep throwing darts until they miss, but they *must* sink at least one enemy ship every round or they get a strike. After five strikes, you're surrounded and it's time to surrender.

Darts Go to War

Darts were played by servicemen and -women in both World Wars, coming to the attention of soldiers who were otherwise unfamiliar with the game. Along with other games like cards, dominoes, draughts, and chess, darts were perfect for wartime conditions, being portable and taking up little space. They were found in recreation huts provided by the YMCA as well as canteens aboard naval ships.

By the time World War II began, darts were standard issue of the British Armed Forces—a set was included in every Navy, Army, and Air Force Institutes (NAAFI) sports pack. The thought was that playing darts helped the soldiers relax, boosted their morale, and took their minds off home. Additionally, servicemen from the United States, Canada, Australia, and New Zealand who were stationed in England and were exposed to the game often took darts home with them, helping to spread this pub pastime to the far reaches of the globe.

A set of NAAFI darts, produced by Dorwin Darts

21 ◎ Record Player Revolution

TURN THE TABLES

HOW TO PLAY

Producing a hit record takes talent, patience, and skill, much like this game of darts. Players rack up points by aiming at the rings of the vinyl. But the game has a catch—there's no room for one-hit wonders: To earn a ring's points, you have to hit it twice in a row. You can take all the time you need, but your turn ends after three consecutive throws without scoring points. Double your points by "climbing the charts"—that is, going from one ring to the next consecutive ring. So if you just scored 5 points and then hit the 10 ring twice, you earn 20 more points! The yellow record label is worth 35 points and the 45 adapter depicted in the center counts, naturally, for 45 points.

No game (or tune) is fun without a bit of risk, so if you hit the playing arm during any of your throws, you'll cause the record to skip and will have to subtract the number of points of the ring beneath the playing arm. Have the highest score after fifteen rounds, and you're golden! For truly ambitious and gifted players, an automatic win can be earned by racking up 300 points in a single turn.

MAKE IT SIMPLER

Pop on your favorite jam band track and earn points with every throw you take. You probably won't miss scoring a point—unless you're throwing pretty wildly—so limit yourself to three throws per turn in this variation. Keep the game going for fifteen minutes or for the duration of the song. The person with the highest number of points at the end of the song is the winner.

TAKE IT UP A NOTCH

Would a true artist settle for a gold record when platinum is within reach? To achieve platinum (and legend) status, rack up 500 points, and *then* be the first person to climb the charts from 5 all the way to the 45 adapter. It's not as easy as it looks. Even if you take an early lead, your opponent still has time to catch up and steal a win if your aim isn't true.

The Fab Bull's-eye

Perhaps one of the strangest and rarest dartboards ever created is the Apple Records board with an apple around the bull's-eye. This dartboard was manufactured to celebrate the founding of the record label, which the Beatles formed in 1968 as a division of Apple Corps Ltd., their multimedia company overseeing recording, publishing, films, electronics, and retail. The band gave out the dartboards as gifts to employees, friends, and music industry folks, but they weren't available for sale to the general public.

Today, officially licensed reproductions (as well as a few unofficial reproductions) are inexpensive and readily found with a quick Internet search. If you want an original, though, prepare for a hunt. Apple Records promotional memorabilia make for some of the most sought-after of the late-period Beatles collectibles. In addition to the board, other promotional items from the Apple Records

Before you ask, no, the entire apple does not count as the bull's-eye.

harvest included watches, Zippo lighters, matchbooks, money clips, playing cards, key chains, and even women's underwear! Then there were the apples themselves—made from wood, granite, glass, rubber, and plush. Nowadays, an original Apple dartboard may set you back at least $1,000.

In a December 2012 auction, Beatle George Harrison's very own board—well-worn from years of playtime—sold for £1,625 (approximately $2,500). Based on the condition of the board, it looked like Harrison was quite good at hitting the 20s, but the bull's-eye didn't have as much wear.

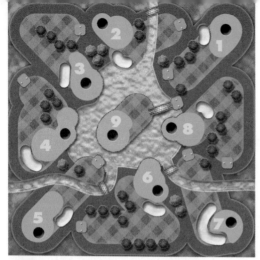

22 ◎ Nine-Hole Golf

FORE!

HOW TO PLAY

On this miniature golf course, players should aim to shoot under par. It's tough, but not altogether impossible. Par for each hole is 4, and you'll want to finish with the lowest score after playing all nine holes. If you land a hole-in-one, you get 1 point. Hitting the green that surrounds each hole counts for an eagle, or 2 points. Landing on the fairway (the checkered green areas) is a birdie and earns 3 points. Watch out for sand traps; they count for 4 points. Missing the hole entirely or landing in a water hazard will get you a bogey, which is 5 points. You can take up to three throws per turn, but only the last dart thrown counts.

If you're happy with your first throw, call it quits on that hole, and sit back until it's your turn on the next hole. Happy putting!

MAKE IT SIMPLER

See who can win the most holes in nine rounds of this game. In each round, take turns throwing at the first hole and go from there, with three throws per person. The lowest score of your three throws counts. In the event of a tie on any of the holes, play it again with a one-throw shoot-out to determine a winner.

TAKE IT UP A NOTCH

Golfers don't get do-overs, and neither should you. For every hole in this game, you only get one shot. Each turn, play three of the nine holes in numerical order. Once you reach the ninth hole, play it twice, and then work your way back down to the first hole, making it a full 18-hole game of golf. Then head off to the clubhouse for a tall Arnold Palmer (a tasty mix of ice tea and lemonade, named after the famous golfer).

GOLF WITH A TRADITIONAL DARTBOARD

A version of golf can be played on any traditional British-style dartboard. Numbers 1 to 18 on the board represent the 18 holes on a golf course. In each round, players aim at one of the numbers. Hitting a single will earn 4 points (par), a triple will earn 3 (a birdie), and the double will earn 2 (an eagle). Missing the board entirely is 5 points (a bogey). The inner bull's-eye is a hole-in-one, though the outer bull is an intimidating 6 points (a double-bogey). Whoever has the lowest score after 18 rounds is the winner, but ties can be settled by shooting for the lowest scores at 19 and 20 as sudden-death holes. Give it a shot and see how it compares to this 9-hole board.

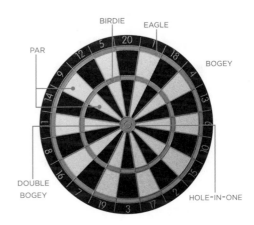

Stateside Darts

One of the most prestigious darts competitions in the United States is the North American Open Darts Tournament, created by Tom Fleetwood in 1970 (Fleetwood would go on to found the American Darts Organization in 1976). The competition entailed men's singles and doubles matches playing best out of three games of 301. Players were required to double in and double out in these matches, meaning the players had all but lost if they couldn't double in right away.

British players didn't compete in the North American Open until 1974, when they were surprised by the fierce competition they faced and they only won the doubles round. World Champ John Lowe called the tournament "the hardest and most difficult one to win."

The tournament wouldn't switch its format to 501, bringing it in line with British competitions, until the early twenty-first century.

23 ◎

Battle of the Drums

MARCH TO YOUR OWN BEAT

HOW TO PLAY

Don't believe anybody who tells you differently: The true backbone of a band is the drummer. They provide the rhythm that establishes everything that comes after. A drummer can't falter, and neither can you when playing this game. Prove you have what it takes to make it as a rock star drummer by matching beats with an opponent. Determine the thrower by tossing a coin, taking turns shooting at a single target, or any other way you come up with.

The game begins with the thrower shooting six darts at the board. Write down which targets the thrower hits and in what order. Then, taking turns, match that beat exactly. Each time you complete the drumbeat perfectly, you earn a point. If you miss even one target, your turn is over. The first person to earn 15 points wins the round.

But the game isn't over just yet. Now it's the other player's turn to lay down the beat. Play to 15 again. If the same player wins both rounds, it's game over. But if it's a tie, settle things with a sudden-death drum battle, in which the players alternate setting the beat and matching it until someone misses. The winner scores a record contract and an international tour. The loser can go along, but only as a roadie.

MAKE IT SIMPLER

If this is your first time in the drummer's seat, here's a good variation to get you warmed up. Try calling out a number, using up to three throws to make it. If you do, your opponent must then match it in three shots or he gets a strike. If you don't make your shot, or if your opponent matches it, he gets to call a shot of his own for you to match within three throws. The first person to get five strikes loses, and will need to head back to band camp for more lessons.

TAKE IT UP A NOTCH

Most drummers use two hands. But you

only use one to throw a dart. With that in mind, try a much more difficult but rewarding variation, a tribute to Rick Allen, the one-armed drummer from Def Leppard. Use your opposite hand (righties go leftie, and vice versa) to rack up the most points over fifteen rounds, with three throws per turn. Each drum piece's value is based on the number it's assigned. Double your score by matching the three shots your opponent made before you. The highest score after the fifteenth round is the winner.

Alter Egos

Just like any good band needs a kick-ass name, every professional darts player needs a great nickname. Here are what the best of the best go by:

Bob Anderson—"The Limestone Cowboy"

Steve Beaton—"The Bronzed Adonis"

Eric Bristow—"The Crafty Cockney"

Matt Chapman—"Baby-Faced Assassin"

Alan Caves—"The Caveman"

Anastasia Dobromyslova (*above*)—"From Russia with Love"

Alan Evans—"The Welsh Wizard"

Les Fitton—"The Natural"

Andy Fordham—"The Viking"

Bobby George—"Mister Glitter," "The King of Darts," and/or "The King of Bling"

Rod Harrington—"The Prince of Style"

Mark Holden—"Top Banana"

John Lowe—"Old Stoneface"

Wayne Mardle—"Hawaii 501"

Dale Newton—"The Artful Dodger"

Kevin Painter—"The Artist"

Phil Taylor (*above*)—"The Power"

Raymond van Barneveld—"Barney"

Vincent van der Voort—"The Dutch Destroyer" (previously known as "Grease Lightning")

Tricia Wright—"The Wright Stuff"

24 ◎ The Beehive
A BUZZ-WORTHY CHALLENGE

HOW TO PLAY

It is man versus insect as you try to gather as much honey as you can in ten rounds. The bees might have stingers, but you have darts! With three throws per turn, aim for the patches of honey and honeycomb. Your aim needs to be perfect—landing anywhere on the hive other than the honey is likely to upset the worker drones. Every three times you hit the hive during the game, you lose 5 points. And any direct hit on one of the drones is going to get you stung, costing you 10 points. Too many bee stings—5 to be exact—is going to trigger your heretofore unknown bee allergy, causing you to swell up and be removed from the game. You're

probably thinking, "Well, I'll just avoid the bees." You could, but then you'd miss out on their freshly gathered buckets of honey, which are worth a whopping 50 points each. To score that big, a little sting or two might be worth it. The highest score after ten rounds wins, but if you slip into negative points at any time in the game, it's an automatic loss.

MAKE IT SIMPLER

Wouldn't it be much easier to take the honey if the bees weren't around? This variation requires you to drive them away before you begin scoring. You can only earn points after you've hit each of the bees three times. Since you'll need at least three rounds to get rid of the bees, stretch this game out from ten to fifteen rounds. But don't let that be an excuse to take your time. The longer you take to hit the bees, the less time you have to score actual points. So get those darts in the air and give those bees a taste of their own medicine with your magnetic, blunt-tipped stinger!

TAKE IT UP A NOTCH

After so many trips back to the hive, the bees have gotten angry, and a bit more proactive. So now it's score or get stung in this adventure in honey theft. Anytime you miss the honey or the honeycomb, deduct 5 points from your score (and deduct 10 if you land a direct hit on a bee). Since you're starting with zero points, you risk losing the game with your very first throw, so it's wise to play "best out of five" when playing this variation. Each game goes to ten rounds, if you can hold out that long, and whoever has the most point wins. Otherwise, the last person left standing is the winner.

Philadelphia: U.S. Darts Epicenter

Just as Philadelphia was the epicenter for the American debut of darts in the 1900s, it was also where the sport had a rebirth in the 1970s, when the traditional British-style dartboard finally took hold in the United States. Charlie Young is renowned for being the first person to hang a British board in his tavern, the Silver Bar, in the late 1960s.

Already a top American-style player, Young and his wife, Alice, became great leaders for the sport over the decades, helping promote British-style darts players and competitions.

They owned another tavern, the Manor, in northeast Philadelphia, which served as a place where players such as Helen Scheerbaum, one of the top female American players of British-style darts, were able to get their start.

One of the most famous stories about Charlie Young is closely tied to another darts tradition that grew out of Philadelphia. Players were known to keep the points of their darts in raw potatoes, a practice that made the tip slicker to help it stick to the board better (Note: For those of you thinking about

jabbing potatoes with darts, please know that dipping them in water will make them just as slick). When he was young, Charlie ate his opponent's potato in order to "psych out" the player.

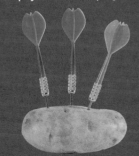

Name one other sport where you can eat a piece of your equipment.

_____

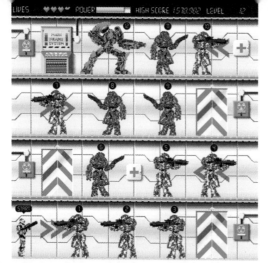

25 ◎ Super Arcade Challenge

DON'T FORGET YOUR QUARTERS

HOW TO PLAY

The 16-bit green gangster Dr. Seismic has declared war on the United Planets, and now it's up to you to stop him in this darts game that hearkens back to coin-op arcade adventures from yesteryear. With three throws per turn—like starting with three lives in a video game—fight your way through Dr. Seismic's army of robotic henchmen, level by level, from the ground up. You must clear the robots on each floor in order to advance. The blue robots are your basic, run-of-the-mill drones that will shut down with just one hit. Those red mecha soldiers are a bit more resilient and are going to require three hits. Once they've been deactivated, you still need to get the elevator going in order to get up to the next level. Hit the red generator box beside the elevator once and then the elevator doors twice to advance to the next floor (if you can't make it in a single turn, pick up where you left off on your next turn).

MAKE IT SIMPLER

Most video games come with adjustable difficulty settings and this one is no exception. When playing on Easy Mode, both blue and red robots only require one hit, and there's a manual override on the elevator, so you can advance to the next level by simply hitting the doors once. Once you make it to the top, hit Dr. Seismic three times to win the game.

TAKE IT UP A NOTCH

Once you've completed the game, you'll want to try the second mission, which is a bit harder than the first. This time around, Dr. Seismic and his robot army are capable of self-repair, so they'll be offline only momentarily. In order to shut them down for good, you'll need to destroy the Main Frame System. Accomplish this by hitting its adjacent generator box once and then the Main

Frame itself twice in a single turn. Don't think that wraps up the game, though. . . . By the time you shut it down, Dr. Seismic and company will have managed to complete repairs, and you'll need to deactivate them again as you make your way out of the building, going back down each level the same way you came in.

The Digital Age

The electronic dartboard was invented in 1975 by Rudy Allison, an American who took a liking to the game during a trip to Ireland. Using soft-tipped darts, players shot at a board comprised of 9,776 tiny holes (much like the board you'll use to play Over/Under on page 15), and their score was automatically recorded thanks to a sensor pad behind each hole, which registered the pressure when the tip of the dart penetrated the board. Initially, these boards shared the same dimensions as a regular dartboard, but the double and triple rings were

The electronic dartboard resembles a honeycomb, with its thousands of scoring holes.

eventually expanded to facilitate higher scoring. The original electronic boards could record up to eight players at once and came preprogrammed with a wide variety of games. These dartboards found much success in the United States, with both coin-operated versions used in bars and the amusement industry, and smaller home versions. They've since spread to Japan where they've been met with much enthusiasm.

However, electronic dartboards and their soft-tipped darts have not received a warm reception in the U.K. All attempts to launch and promote the coin-operated boards have failed. The British are justifiably proud of inventing darts and resist unnecessary improvements to their creation. In addition, games of darts have always been free in pubs, so the notion of paying to play the coin-operated version is of little interest.

26 ◎ Bowling
KING OF THE ALLEY

HOW TO PLAY

There's no greater symbol of status than a private bowling alley. And now you have one! So try racking up the highest score after ten rounds. You have two throws per round, but if you land on a strike or a spare with your first throw, you forfeit your second throw. And if you hit a number on your first throw and strike on your second, sorry, but it counts as a spare. Each pin has two values, depending where your dart lands, so aim carefully.

Just as in real bowling, the values of spares and strikes are determined by your next turn. Keep a pad of paper handy for some quick calculations. If you land on a spare, you determine your score by adding 10 points to the first throw of your next turn. For example, if you land on a 7 after getting a spare, your score for that spare will be 17. You determine the score of your strike by adding 10 to your next two throws—so if you hit 6 and 7 on your next turn, your score for the strike would be 6 + 7 + 10, or 23. Throwing a perfect game, twelve strikes in a row, is equal to 300 points. Throwing all spares is worth 150, but if you're that good with your aim, why aren't you throwing for the strike?

Remember, if you hit a spare on your last round, you get an extra throw, and if you hit a strike, you get two extra throws. Some might ask, "What if you just keep throwing strikes? Do you have to keep playing forever?" The short answer is "Yes."

MAKE IT SIMPLER

Use only the higher point values on each pin, no matter where your dart lands. And spares are just worth a straight 10 points (no adding points from your next turn) and strikes are worth 15.

TAKE IT UP A NOTCH

For a tougher variation, players are required to hit a pin twice during their turn in order to score off it. This means you'll now have four throws instead of two, but the likelihood of scoring each turn is decreased.

BOWLING WITH A TRADITIONAL DARTBOARD

A version of bowling can be played on a traditional British-style dartboard, with the 20 segment on the board serving as your bowling lane. Once again, you only use two darts per turn. Hitting the triple ring equals 10 pins. The double ring is 9 pins. The inner single is 3 and the outer single is 7. You earn 2 extra points if you hit a triple and a double, and an extra 10 points if you hit two triples. So if you throw a perfect game, your final total will be 300 points, just like in bowling.

Mixed Matches

Combining bowling and darts doesn't seem like that much of a stretch when you consider this odd pairing in darts history: In July 1977, famed boxer Muhammad Ali played an exhibition darts match against former Welsh champ Alan Evans at the Gypsy's Green Stadium in South Shields, a town in northeast England. Evans was one of the top darts players in the world at the time, and to even the match, he played under handicap rules, only scoring points by hitting triples. Ali managed to win the game by hitting the bull's-eye, and promptly declared himself "Darts Champion of the World."

Muhammed Ali (top front of bus) was met with much fanfare during his trip to England's northeast.

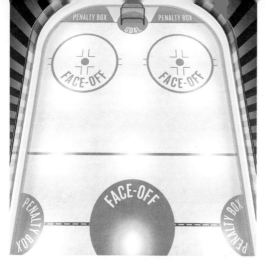

27 ⊙ Hockey Face-off

HAT-TRICK TIME

HOW TO PLAY

Finally, a version of hockey that doesn't require ice skates, Rollerblades, or any other balance-impairing footwear. Launch into this game by taking turns aiming at the blue face-off circle (aka the center ice) until someone misses. The winner of the face-off gets the puck and can begin scoring points by aiming for the goal. To score a point, you need to hit the goal three times. This rule may sound tough, but there's no room for wimps in hockey. Don't worry if your throws land elsewhere on the ice. The puck is yours until you lose it—that is, it's yours unless you land in a penalty box and have to forfeit your turn, or if you hit any of the three face-off circles, at which point you and your opponent need to start taking turns throwing at the blue center ice again until someone misses. Your number of goal hits does not carry over from turn to turn, so if you hit it twice and then wind up in the penalty box, you're starting from scratch when you get the puck again.

Be careful with those visits to the penalty box—if you're sent to the penalty box three times, your opponent earns a power play, meaning they can keep the puck the next time they land in a face-off circle or a penalty box; think of it as a "get out of jail free" card. And if you're sent to the penalty box six times, then you've just handed them the game, because you're getting ejected. Barring that, the first player to earn 20 points is the winner. Next stop, the Stanley Cup!

MAKE IT SIMPLER

You're already risking a trip to the penalty box with every single throw at the goal. Take a breather by requiring only one hit in the goal to score a point. Additionally, though you can still be sent to the penalty box, you no longer have to worry about being ejected from the game. Instead, after six trips to the penalty box, your opponent just receives a power play. Think pee-wee league hockey. Have fun out there!

TAKE IT UP A NOTCH

Scoring a goal starts to seem like a cinch when there's no goalie blocking you. Test your finesse by placing a dart directly in front of the goal (just outside its red circle). Goalies tend to move around, so feel free to attempt to knock the dart out of the way by hitting it. You only have to put it back once your turn is over. Otherwise it's an open goal while you have the puck.

A Line Is Drawn

Why is the throwing line for darts called the "oche"? It's derived from the word *hockey* and pronounced the same—just without the *h*. You're probably thinking, "Huh? Isn't that another sport altogether?" Well, we're not talking about that hockey. The throwing line was allegedly created by placing three beer crates between the dartboard and the player. These crates were from the brewing company Hockey & Sons. Each crate was 3 feet long, creating a throwing distance of 9 feet. At least that's what most people will tell you. Another possible origin of

Darryl Fitton goes toe-to-toe with the oche at the 2010 World Professional Darts Championship.

"oche" is the word *hocken*, which means to spit. Many Victorian pubs held spitting contests, which involved standing behind a line and trying to spit the farthest.

According to the *Oxford English Dictionary*, *hockey* was a corruption of the word "hog-line," which was the distance-line a stone must cross in order to count in the game of curling. The reality of the situation is that the origin of the word hockey remains unknown, but it was used by other pub games to include a point from which the player would throw and it was adopted for darts.

Over the years, the regulation distance of the oche has varied between 6 and 9 feet, until the World Darts Federation recommended a distance of 7 feet 9¼ inches in 1977. The oche has stood firm ever since.

28 ◎ *Football*

PASS THE PIGSKIN

HOW TO PLAY

This is the perfect darts game for Sunday afternoons and Monday nights. Imagine playing football without all the padding, or the huge guys knocking you over. This game boils down football to the essentials (including an end zone dance, if you're so inclined). As with real football, the object of the game is to score points. Touchdowns are worth 6 points and field goals are worth 9. Initially, each player gets only one throw to try to score, but depending on where your dart lands, you can earn extra throws during each of your turns. If your dart lands between the 50- and the 40-yard lines, you earn four more chances; between the

40 and the 30, three chances; between the 30 and the 20, two chances; and between the 20 and the 10, one chance. Once you score or run out of shots, the next player is up. If you land on an interception, your turn is over, no matter how many shots you have left. And watch out for too many careless throws into the crowded stadium. It will earn you a penalty. After five penalties, you'll be thrown out of the game! Whoever has the highest score after a set period of time—sixteen to twenty minutes is generally recommended—is headed to the Super Bowl.

MAKE IT SIMPLER

Take on the role of a running back and get that football up to the goalpost. Starting at the 50-yard line, advance 10 yards per throw. You can keep going until you miss the next yard line (or overshoot it). When it's your turn again, you have to start back at the 50-yard line. Once you've reached the 10-yard line, shoot for the 6-point touchdown or the 9-point field goal. You'll have three shots to make it before your turn is up and the other team gets the ball. The player with the highest score after sixteen minutes is the winner.

TAKE IT UP A NOTCH

Welcome to the Super Bowl (half-time show not included). Once again you're advancing up the field, but in order to gain 10 yards, you need to do it three times in a row. If you make it, you have three more throws for the next 10 yards. If you miss, your turn is over and you can try again the next time you're up. Once you've reached the 10-yard line, both the 6-point touchdown and the 9-point field goal will need to be hit three times to earn the points. Be careful about landing on an interception, which will cut short your chance of scoring. An interception will also give your opponent a chance to throw from the 10-yard line before being sent back to the 50-yard line to begin their turn.

A Royal Game

We've already dispelled those rumors about King Henry VIII and darts (see page 23), but that doesn't mean British royalty and the game have never crossed paths. In December 1937, King George VI and Queen Elizabeth played a short game of darts while visiting a social club in Slough, Buckinghamshire (a town Americans might know as the setting of the original U.K. television series *The Office*). The game occurred after the queen was quoted as saying, "Do let me try. I have heard so much about this game." They both threw three darts each, and the queen beat her husband 21 points to 19 (she was, however, standing a foot closer to the dartboard). As brief as this game was, the nation took notice, particularly women. In the *Sunday Chronicle*, the queen was credited with making British women "darts-conscious" in an article

Her Majesty the Queen played a round as factory workers and clerks looked on.

with a headline that read: "Women Flock to Follow the Queen's Lead at Darts."

you must decide whether you're happy with it or want to continue on (unless it's your third throw, of course).

The game ends after the ninth round, with the highest scorer as the winner. If you need more of a challenge, require players to hit a target three times during their turn.

29 ⊚ **Skee-Ball**
YOU'RE ON A ROLL

HOW TO PLAY

If there ever was a game more under-appreciated than darts, it would be Skee-Ball. Now this unsung staple of the Jersey Shore, among other places, gets a little time to shine with this dartboard variation. The object of this classic arcade game is to "roll" the highest score. But instead of rolling balls up an incline, you must use the darts to hit the numbers over nine rounds.

To score points, aim for each of the target holes. Each target has a fairly large scoring area (and they get larger as the point values decrease), so stand back at least 8 feet. You can throw up to three darts per round, but only the last one counts, so after each throw

The Voice of Darts

COMMENTATOR SID WADDELL was known as the "Voice of Darts," having spent nearly forty years covering darts matches. His colorful, witty words made him one of the most unforgettable figures in the sport. Waddell passed away in 2012, leaving behind a legacy few, if any, could match. Here's just a small sample of Waddell's words:

"The atmosphere is a cross between the Munich Beer Festival and the Coliseum when the Christians were on the menu!"

"That was like throwing three pickled onions into a thimble."

"If you had to throw a knife at your wife in the circus, you'd want to throw it like that."

"There's only one word for that—magic darts!"

30 ◎ **Global Conqueror**
WORLD SERIES

HOW TO PLAY

Finally, a chance to take over the world! Make history by conquering the globe, region by region, before your opponent. With three throws per turn, begin your conquest by targeting the zones. In order to take over a zone, you need to hit it three times. You don't have to land all three hits in the same turn and you don't need to conquer one zone before moving on to the next. You can keep track on a scorecard. If you're truly determined, aim directly for a zone command center and hit it twice in a single round for an immediate takeover.

At some point, you're going to have to go to war with your opponent in order to steal their

zones. To do so, you'll need to hit their zone command center three times in a single turn. The first person to claim all the zones wins.

A simpler game is to race your opponents to claiming all the zones. Players can claim the same zones, so there's no going to war, but only the person who gets to all five first can keep them!

31 ⊚ *Roulette*

GIVE IT A SPIN

HOW TO PLAY

Taking risks can pay off in roulette—how much is up to you. In this game, back up your throwing skills with a wager at each turn. Every player begins with 50 points. Each turn, players must call a shot and then make it within three throws. As in roulette, you have multiple betting options. You can bet on just the color or a specific number. If you call a color and hit it, you win 5 points. But if you call a number, or the bull's-eye, and hit it, you win 10 points. Feel free to call odds or evens, and if the number is what you called, take 2 points. Keep in mind that if you miss, you lose the points you bet, and you can only bet with what you

have available. As long as you're on a winning streak, this won't be a problem. But if you're down to 5 points, then you can only call the color or odds/evens. If you hit a 0 or 00, you get no points and lose your turn. Once per game you can opt to borrow from the house by hitting a bull's-eye twice in a turn, though you only get to keep 5 of the 10 points you'd usually earn by hitting it. But if you miss, no points are deducted. The first player to pull in 250 points, or get his opponent down to zero, wins the game.

MAKE IT SIMPLER

Betting should always be done responsibly, or perhaps not at all. Keep it a friendly game by shooting for the highest number of points each turn, once again starting by calling your target. If you call a color, then you score 5 points each time you hit it. If you call a number or the bull's-eye, score 10 points each time. If you're playing odds/evens, you earn 2 points for each dart that lands. The highest score after 15 rounds is the winner.

TAKE IT UP A NOTCH

Only expert gamblers should play this version of the game, in which you wager against your opponent instead of the house. Start off with some extra playing "money"—100 points each. When you're up, call your shot and then take up to three shots to make it. If you succeed, you'll receive the 2, 5, or 10 points from your opponent, but if you miss, you'll have to pay them out. The first person to get 250 points is the winner, unless their opponent goes broke first.

What Are the Odds?

Meet Olly Croft, the man largely responsible for the darts boom of the 1970s and '80s. A tile worker from London and an avid darts player, Croft had high aspirations for the sport. In 1973, he and some like-minded individuals started the British Darts Organisation (BDO) out of his living room. This democratic committee became the recognized governing body for darts, creating the rules and guidelines that still govern how the game is played today. Croft also saw the potential for darts to be a televised sport. With matches airing on the BBC and ITV, darts players became superstars in the championships Croft organized.

After conquering Britain, Croft helped establish the World Darts Federation in 1976 to link the worldwide organizations under one umbrella and foster international recognition for darts as a sport. The organization began with fourteen nations and has grown to include seventy.

Croft left an indelible mark, despite the televised darts bubble bursting in the 1980s and the break in ranks with the BDO that led to the formation of the Professional Darts Corporation (a separate governing organization). In recognition of his contributions, Croft received the esteemed distinction of OBE (Officer of the Most Excellent Order of the British Empire) from Queen Elizabeth II in 2004.

Darts visionary Olly Croft

Raceway Melee

START YOUR ENGINES!

HOW TO PLAY

Think you can make a lap around one of the toughest racetracks there is? With three throws per turn, start with racecar #1 and proceed to hit each car in numerical order to complete the winding course. To move from one car to the next, you need to hit it three times. With the start of each new turn, continue throwing where you left off.

You'll have to be quick to swerve around those oil slicks—landing on one will cause you to lose control and set you back one car. If your aim is sharp, take a shot at the Pass arrows—they will let you jump ahead a car. (Note: You can shoot at any of the Pass arrows at any time, not just the one closest to your car.) But watch out for the crash sites; landing on one of those will send you all the way back to racecar #1. No game is complete until you cross the finish line, hitting it three times.

The first person to complete the lap takes home the trophy! Extra laps are always available if you're feeling ambitious and want to keep the game going longer. Or for a quicker game, with multiple laps, try shooting car to car, one dart for each, in a game of five laps.

More Words from the Voice of Darts

THERE WERE SO MANY GEMS THAT CAME FROM commentator Sid Waddell (see page 54), limiting them to four would be a shame. Here are some other favorite lines from Waddell's years in darts:

"That's the greatest comeback since Lazarus."

"He's been burning the midnight oil at both ends."

"He looks about as happy as a penguin in a microwave."

"It's like trying to pin down a kangaroo on a trampoline."

"Even Hypotenuse would have trouble working out these angles."

"He's about as predictable as a wasp on speed."

33 ◎ Knockdown

TIME FOR A SHOOT-OFF

HOW TO PLAY

Grab a pellet gun and down all the flags in a row before your opponent can. A flag is knocked down after you hit it three times, or, for sharpshooters, by hitting the triple bar once, or the double bar and the single. Then land a dart on the flag's bull's-eye and it's down for the count. You don't need to knock down a number before moving on to the next. Keep track of your numbers with a scorecard.

To determine who takes the top row and who takes the bottom, shoot for the highest score with three darts (the doubles bar will double the score, and the triples will triple it). The player with the highest score gets to pick which row he or she wants.

Practice your aim in preparation for this game by playing a variation in which you're shooting for the highest score after ten rounds. Once again, have a single round to determine who gets the top and bottom rows. Whoever has the bottom will have a slight advantage with the higher point value. Bull's-eyes on both rows count for 25 points. Increase the challenge by requiring players to match or beat their previous turn's score for each of the rounds in order to earn points. If you set the bar too high with three bull's-eyes in your first turn, you'll have quite a difficult game ahead of you.

Showing Off

"EVERYONE LOVES A PENALTY SHOOT-OUT AT THE END of a football match, right? Well, there's a penalty shoot-out every two or three minutes in a game of darts."

—Eric Bristow, on the intensity of the sport

Bristow had a distinctive style, with his pinky finger sticking straight up as he threw (see page 17). But the dainty throw didn't have anything to do with all his wins. Toward the end of his career, he admitted it was just for show.

Please Stand By

BOOB TUBE BATTLE

HOW TO PLAY

The series finale of your favorite TV show is about to begin, but your DVR is busted and the cable company keeps putting you on hold. If you don't watch, you'll never be able to show your face (or avatar) on any of your favorite social media websites later tonight. It's time to break out the rabbit-ear antenna and see what sort of signal you can pick up. Tune in by being the first person to score 500 points, with three darts per turn. Refer to the handy color bar at the bottom of the screen to help guide you in your struggle to survive as a digital kid trapped in an analog world. All darts that land outside the circles count for zero. Don't overshoot: To win, you need exactly 500 points, otherwise you'll have blown right past your show and landed on that static-riddled channel showing a telenovela. Every point you go over 500 will be subtracted from your score at the start of the next round. For example, if you have 490 points and hit a 25 zone, you must subtract the 15-point overage and wind up with 475 points. Keep that in mind when aiming for the high-value colors as your points accumulate. They're helpful when you're first trying to rack up points, but can quickly get you into a lot of trouble. Fingers crossed you make it before the opening credits end!

MAKE IT SIMPLER

All you're trying to do is relax with your favorite TV show after a long day at work, so let's lower the stakes. Try getting to that 500 without worrying about going over—575 is just as impressive as 500 in most people's eyes. In addition, earn a 100-point bonus if you hit any four of the five red 100-point zones. How's that for incentive?

TAKE IT UP A NOTCH

Some shows are worth a little extra effort, so why not try a trickier variation of the game, and revisit the classic 501 darts game? In order to win, players must double out. That's right; you must hit the same point-value twice while reaching that exact 500-point mark. So if your score is 450, you'll need to hit two 25s. Just think how good you'll feel when you land that double out and can finally kick up your feet and watch some TV!

Darts on Your TV

Bullseye, a British game show that aired from 1981 to 1995 and again in 2006, combined dart throwing and trivia questions. The show pitted three pairs of contestants (one to throw darts and one to answer questions) against each other for three rounds. During the first round, players would throw at a board marked with categories, with the questions increasing in difficulty according to their prize value. From there, players went to the second round, in which they would throw darts at a traditional board. The highest-scoring teams could then answer questions to earn more money.

Only the pair with the highest score advanced to the third and final round, where they threw at a black-and-red prize board. For every red segment they hit, they'd win a prize. Before heading home, the pair was offered a chance to gamble their winnings against the mystery Star Prize. If they chose to do so, they had to score 101 points on a traditional dartboard with six darts (three darts for each member of the pair). Pairs who made it received prizes such as vacations, cars, or speedboats.

Toward the end of its first run, the show was receiving 12,000 contestant applications a year and there was a five-year studio audience waiting list.

On the set of Bullseye

35 ⊙ *Coney Island Hustle*

WIN A PRIZE, ANY PRIZE!

HOW TO PLAY

No trip to Coney Island is complete until you try your luck at a boardwalk game. In this carnival classic, see if you can score more points than your friends in fifteen rounds, with three throws per round. In order to score off a balloon, you must hit the balloon three times in a single turn.

Up the difficulty by popping balloons, meaning your opponent can't score points on them if you've hit them three times. (However, you can continue to score off that balloon if you choose to do so.) Both you and your opponent can opt to re-inflate a popped balloon by hitting it three times in a turn, but you won't score any points for those hits.

Change up the game a little bit by earning points whenever you hit any three balloons with the same point value in a single turn. Your options get more limited as the point values go up. There are plenty of 1s and 5s, but only five 10s, three 25s, and two 50s. You can still choose to pop a balloon with three hits in a single turn, giving your opponent fewer targets as the game continues into the later rounds.

A League of Their Own

AS TELEVISION COVERAGE AND sponsorship interest of darts matches declined in the 1980s, many professional players felt the British Darts Organisation was simply not doing enough for the sport. So in 1993, a group of sixteen players—including top stars like Eric Bristow and John Lowe—broke rank and started their own organization, the World Darts Council, which was later renamed the Professional Darts Corporation. Both groups now have their own world championships, as well as different areas of focus.

6 ◎ Haunted House

BOO! (WHAT? THAT WASN'T SCARY?)

HOW TO PLAY

This decrepit house needs an exorcist. Otherworldly entities have taken over, and it's up to you to drive them away with your top-of-the-line paranormal extermination darts! The object of the game is to earn the most points by taking out as many supernatural creatures as you can in fifteen minutes of gameplay.

You've got three throws per turn. Each successful hit on a ghost will earn you 1 point. Landing a hit on the witch or either of the tombstones is worth 5 points. Those eerie red and blue glowing lights coming from the attic are worth 10, so start aiming for those windows if you really want to up your score. Targets can be used again and again, so keep throwing until your ghost-busting time is up, and add 50 points to your final score if you've managed to hit every ghastly target during the course of the game. Any stray shots that hit the house will cost you 3 points. The property value is already plummeting thanks to the haunting. Further damage to the house isn't going to help it.

High Roller

PROFESSIONAL DARTS DUDE Adrian Lewis is known as "Jackpot." The British player earned the nickname while competing in the 2005 Las Vegas Desert Classic. During a casino visit in his off-time, he played a slot machine and hit an incredible $72,000 jackpot. But Lewis was twenty years old at the time, a year shy of the legal gambling age in the United States. In addition to being unable to collect the prize money, he just narrowly avoided being arrested. Fortunately, he had a promising darts career to fall back on. Lewis went on to win the Professional Darts Corporation World Championship twice, in 2011 and in 2012.

37 ◎ Blackjack

HIT ME AGAIN

HOW TO PLAY

There's no way to count cards in this version of Blackjack. Just like in the playing card game, the object here is to get as close as you can to 21 points without going bust (i.e., going over 21). Each face card (the king, the queen, and the jack) counts for 10 and the ace counts for either 11 or 1, your choice. To begin a game, each player throws two darts. Depending on the cards you hit, you can either "stand," meaning you're happy with your two cards and don't want another, or you can "hit," by throwing for a third card. You're not playing against a dealer and you can see all of your opponent's cards, so you need not worry about the usual strategy of figuring out when to stand and when to hit. Just aim carefully, because if you're off, you risk hitting a card that will make you bust. Alternating turns, the first person to win ten "hands" will walk away the champ.

MAKE IT SIMPLER

If you want to ease this game up a bit, simply throw for the highest cards each round. Or call a suit and throw at that until you miss, keeping score by seeing how many of the suit you hit.

◎ OR PLAY THIS: POKER

You have an entire deck of cards, so you might want to play some other card games. Why not try some poker? Each round, players must shoot for the best hand of five cards with five throws. If you're not familiar with all the different poker hands, here's a quick rundown:

The highest hand is a royal flush, five cards in sequence of the same suit, starting with a ten, continuing through the face cards, with an ace as the high card. The second highest hand is a straight flush, any five cards in sequence of the same suit. Then comes four of a kind, with four cards of the same rank, followed by the full house (three of a kind and a pair); the flush (five of the same suit);

the straight (any five in sequence, not all of the same suit); three of a kind (three of the same rank); two pairs (two pairs of matching ranks); and one pair (a pair of matching rank).

If you prefer the Texas Hold'em style of poker, you can play that here as well. For two players, you must establish the five community cards by taking turns throwing. These cards will be used by both of you. Players then must throw for their own two private cards, also known as "hole" cards. Keeping the community cards in mind, you're going to make the best possible five-card hand when throwing for your two cards.

See who can win the most hands in ten rounds of the game!

Darts All-Stars

In 2000, when *Sports Illustrated* named the fifty greatest athletes from each of the fifty states, only one professional darts player made the list: Stacy Bromberg (*left*), from Las Vegas, Nevada. Within the American Darts Organization, she has been ranked the No. 1 women's player an incredible record sixteen times, thirteen of which were consecutive years! Following that, she won the World Darts Federation World Cup Women's Championship in 2009 and the Professional Darts Corporation's first ever Women's World Championship in 2010.

In addition to being one of the top-ranked players for over a decade, she has also raised more than $100,000 for the Make-A-Wish Foundation of Southern Nevada through her own organization, Scoring for Charity. Due to her charity work, Stacy has earned the nickname "The Wish Granter."

Lest you need any more reasons to think Stacy is awesome, for a day job, she works as a private investigator, and she drives a white Mustang with the license plate A1DARTR. Stacy, you're fabulous!

Stacy Bromberg, numero uno!

38 ◉ Picky Pizza

EXTRA CHEESE, PLEASE

HOW TO PLAY

This game is easy as (pizza) pie. Apologies if that joke was too cheesy. Your favorite pizza place is usually reliable, but this time they messed up. You ordered a large half pepperoni/half mushroom pizza, but were delivered a pizza with the toppings mixed together! You and your friends are much too hungry to wait for another pizza to arrive. You're going to have to pick off what you don't want, so you might as well make a game of it. Pretend those darts are little forks and have a go at it. One player or team has to remove the meat, while the other gets rid of the fungus. You get three throws per round to target the toppings. Each pepperoni or mushroom is worth 4 points, but if you call the slice of pizza at which you're aiming, you'll earn double the points. Once you've picked all your topping targets off a slice, it's yours and your opponent cannot score off of it. (You'll need to keep a pad nearby to keep track of your successfully "removed" toppings.) While slices are still in play, landing on a pepperoni or mushroom that has already been hit during the game will earn you just 2 points. That little plastic "pizza saver" in the center that keeps the cheese from sticking to the top of the box isn't worth any points, so in a rare twist for a darts game, you're not going to be aiming for a bull's-eye. The player with the highest score after fifteen rounds wins.

MAKE IT SIMPLER

Sometimes you just want a plain cheese pizza. Even among the most adventurous eaters, it's been known to happen. In this case, score points by throwing for any toppings over fifteen rounds. Every topping you hit is worth the point value of the slice's number.

TAKE IT UP A NOTCH

Let's bring that white plastic pizza saver into play. It's a bit bigger than any of the toppings, so try hitting it before you start scoring points each turn. You now have three throws to hit the plastic, and another three to aim for your toppings. Your throws don't carry over from the saver to the toppings, so if you hit the saver with your first or second throw, you still only have three more throws to score points during that turn.

Another variation is to place dibs on certain slices. Shoot for every other slice. The same scoring applies: 4 points for hitting your target for the first time, and 2 for hitting it again, but if you hit a topping on a slice that isn't yours, you lose 4 points. The game is over when you've hit all of your toppings. In the event of a tie finish, the person with the highest score wins.

Healthy Competition

With its origins in pub culture, playing darts has often gone hand in hand with drinking alcohol and smoking cigarettes. The stereotypical darts player was famously skewered in 1980 on the British sketch comedy series *Not the Nine O'Clock News*. In the sketch, fictitious players Guy "Fat Belly" Gutbucket and Tommy "Even Fatter Belly" Belcher (both costumed with greatly exaggerated midsections) pretended to throw darts while drinking excessively, with the 501 scoreboard measuring their level of drunkenness based on downing single pints of lager, double gins, and triple vodkas. Of course the match ended with Guy getting sick. Though it was satire—and great satire at that—the sketch did no favors for the British Darts Organisation (BDO) and its fight to legitimize the game. Players, however, appreciated the humor. In his book *Bellies and Bullseyes: The Outrageous True Story of Darts*, champ Sid Waddell said he believed drinking and smoking were complementary to the players' skills. He felt it "made them human, ordinary, familiar." This sentiment was not shared by the BDO. In the hopes of improving their image and attracting more sponsors, they officially banned drinking and smoking during all televised matches in 1989. Players were encouraged to drink water instead.

three seagulls during the game, you're out (and should probably be banned from the boardwalk permanently)!

If a dart lands in your hat, feel free to cash it in with an extra throw. The highest score after ten rounds is the winner. In addition to keeping track of your score, write down how many balls you managed to hit during each turn. There's a 50-point bonus for every ten balls hit in a turn. And in the event of a tie, the person who has hit the greatest number of balls is the winner.

Boardwalk Juggling

KEEP YOUR BALLS IN THE AIR!

HOW TO PLAY

Show off your juggling skills at a beachside boardwalk—how long can you keep all of the balls in the air? Find out and earn points by throwing at them. Each ball has a different point value between 10 and 75, with the double ring and bull's-eye being worth twice as much. Your turn doesn't end until you miss a ball, so keep those darts flying. Watch out for the pesky seagulls. If you hit one, you'll be slapped with a penalty for cruelty to wildlife and 25 points will be deducted from your score. And if you hit

MAKE IT SIMPLER

The object is still to score as many points as you can, but with only three throws per turn. There's no need to tally up your longest runs, but some new bonuses are in play: If you hit three balls of the same value during a turn (whether it's the same ball three times or different ones), add a bonus ball to your score—for example, if you hit three 10 balls, your score is 40 instead of 30.

TAKE IT UP A NOTCH

Let's make this juggling a little more competitive by requiring players to aim for the balls in consecutive order, either in a clockwise or counter-clockwise circle (you can start with any ball you choose). Like any proficient juggler, you're allowed to switch directions, but you can't skip over any balls without losing your turn. Every full circle you complete adds an extra 100 points to your score, but hitting a seagull now comes with a 100-point penalty. The winner is determined by the highest score after five rounds, or by going around the full circle five times in a single turn. The extra throw from landing on the hat is no longer in play; that would make the game too easy, don't you think?

But Is It a Sport?

As the popularity of darts has grown, so has the argument about its legitimacy as a sport. In 2001, BBC reporter Rob Bonnet stirred up controversy by quoting his father, who said darts isn't a sport because it isn't played with a ball. In defense of darts, former world finalist and fellow BBC pundit Bobby George shot back, "Is ballroom dancing a sport? It's recognized as a sport, but I don't see any balls there."

Bobby and other professional darters finally got their day when Sport England, the country's governing sports agency, officially recognized darts as a sport in 2005. While celebrating this victory, many professional darters, including Phil "The Power" Taylor, set their sights on another goal: seeing darts played at the Olympics. It's not a complete stretch of the imagination. And, as a matter of fact, when the Republic of Yemen produced four sports-related stamps to commemorate the 1964 Olympic Games in Tokyo, they oddly chose two games that were not recognized as Olympic sports—table tennis and darts. The former eventually became an Olympic game in 1998, so perhaps it is only a matter of time for darts!

40 ◎ Word on the Street

SPELL A W-I-N

HOW TO PLAY

Here's a game where a keen ability to spell will help you win—and believe it or not, you may actually expand your vocabulary in the process. The object of the game is to spell a word each round for ten rounds. Each letter of the word you're spelling earns you a point. Get double points if your word includes the letters Q or Z. If you spell a word using both Q and Z, prepare to have a dictionary handy to back up your claim—and triple your score for the round! I know what you're thinking—there are no words with Q *and* Z. Not true, my friend.

"Squeeze" is just one of many. You *don't* get points by spelling names of people, places, brands, etc. Sorry, but proper nouns are off limits!

Take as many throws as you need to complete your word each round, but if you miss a letter, your turn is over. You only score points for full words, but if you complete a short word within the longer one you intended to spell (such as spelling "tumult" while on your way to spelling "tumultuous"), you do get points for the shorter word. Players who manage to successfully spell a word in each of the ten rounds get a 50-point bonus at the end of the game. And if you're truly ambitious, try creating a ten-word sentence with your turns, an achievement that will earn you 100 extra points. Whoever has the highest score after the tenth round should pack their bags and head to the state spelling bee.

MAKE IT SIMPLER

Get rid of the one word per turn rule and spell as many words as you can until you miss. If you flub in the middle of the word, your turn is over, but you can come back to the word at the start of the next round. The 50-point bonus remains if you manage to spell ten words, as well as the 100-point sentence bonus.

TAKE IT UP A NOTCH

This game is already plenty difficult, but you can make it more of a challenge by requiring a minimum number of letters per word in order to score. This may be the time to dust off your SAT vocabulary flash cards. Start with a five-letter minimum, but if that's still too easy, try going up to eight or nine. You can also make a rule prohibiting the same word from being spelled twice. And, no, adding an "s" just to make a word plural won't count either.

Word of the Day

Ever hear of *dartitis*? If you're not a professional darts player, you probably haven't. Fear not, it isn't contagious. It's a psychological condition in which a darts player is physically unable to release the dart. Golf and baseball aficionados may be familiar with the "yips," a similar affliction. Despite research into the condition, no one knows the exact cause of it, and it can affect different players in different ways, afflicting new players as well as those who have been playing for years. The term was coined in 1981 in *Darts World* magazine, but it did not appear in the *Oxford English Dictionary* until 2007. Five-time world champion Eric Bristow (*below*) was one of the first professional players known to suffer from dartitis. He developed it in 1987, the year after the last of his world title victories. Though he eventually recovered, he never quite played the same. He did, however, recover his world title in 1990. There's no known cure for dartitis, but players have found relief through various means, such as adjusting their throwing style, eating better, weight lifting, and swapping their darts for lighter or heavier ones.

Eric Bristow came down with a case of dartitis in 1987.

◉ Additional Reading and Resources

If we did our job right, this book should have whet your appetite for exploring all things darts. To continue your darts education, check out some of these great titles, all of which were invaluable when compiling the history, facts, anecdotes, and records in this book.

The American Darts Organization Book of Darts, Chris Carey, The Lyons Press, 2005.

Bellies and Bullseyes: The Outrageous True Story of Darts, Sid Waddell, Ebury Press, 2007.

The Darts Bible, David Norton and Patrick Mcloughlin with Steve Brown, Chartwell Books, 2010.

Darts in England, 1900–1939: A Social History, Patrick Chaplin, Manchester University Press, 2009.

Darts Miscellany, Matt Bozeat, Pitch Publishing, 2010.

The Little Book of Darts, Brian Belton, The History Press, 2011.

The Official Bar Guide to Darts, Patrick Chaplin, Ph.D., Puzzlewright Press, 2010.

Scoring for Show, Doubles for Dough: Bobby George's Darts Lingo, Bobby George and Dr. Patrick Chaplin, Apex Publishing, 2011.

To the Point: The Story of Darts in America, Dan William Peek, Pebble Publishing, 2001.